Katie Wilson

Computers in Libraries
An Introduction
for Library Technicians

Pre-publication
REVIEWS,
COMMENTARIES,
EVALUATIONS . . .

"*Computers in Libraries* is a comprehensive look at the history, development, and current use of computers in libraries. It provides the reader with a well-balanced perspective from the broad overview level to an understandable level of detail expressed clearly and simply.

The structure of the book enables the reader to move through the context of computers in libraries commencing with the history of computers and their adoption for library work, to the more specific application of computing technology to the tasks in libraries such as serials management, cataloging, and acquisitions.

Each chapter begins with a glossary that demystifies the language and terminology used in that chapter. This is followed by a clear explanation and coverage of the topic of the chapter including references for further reading and exploration. Many of the topics cover a brief historical explanation that gives a good contextual basis for further development of the topic from the broad view to the more specific library application. Review questions at the end of each chapter help readers assess their grasp of the key issues in the chapter and identify any areas for further research on the topic.

Katie Wilson has produced a timely and well-considered text that will be a useful reference on computers in libraries for years to come."

Brenda McConchie, Grad Dip (Advanced Librarianship), AALAI, *Director, Solved at McConchie Pty Ltd.*

More pre-publication
REVIEWS, COMMENTARIES, EVALUATIONS . . .

"*Computers in Libraries* is enlightening, practical in approach, and an essential guide to library technology. In her descriptive and informed text Katie Wilson draws a conceptual map of technology applications and trends in libraries. Yes, library technicians will benefit from the well-organized chapters, each with pertinent terminology defined, visual examples and review questions, but this book is a reference resource for a wider audience. Technical support staff working with libraries will gain insight into the complexity and interrelatedness of library operations, as well as specific applications of technology. New and seasoned librarians will appreciate this single-source opportunity to review and reflect upon the permeation of technology in processes and services.

Computers in Libraries equips the reader with a solid foundation of how and why technology works throughout the full spectrum of library workflow. Current developments such as federated searching and OpenURL are addressed as well as future directions. The author's depth of experience implementing and teaching library technology systems is evident."

Paula Garrett, MS
Library Director, Illinois Mathematics and Science Academy

"Technology savvy librarian, systems trainer, and teacher, Katie Wilson, has accomplished more in *Computers in Libraries* than the subtitle of the book describes. This book takes a stepped approach to all aspects of library automation, organizing the components, and providing a logical explanation, simply, of how it all works. In addition to being an introduction to library automation, the book is also an excellent refresher for all those involved in libraries. It is a timely overview of the matrix of library automation, how it has evolved, what structures and components are critical, and what to expect in the future. By the time you finish reading this fluent and well-organized overview of computers in libraries, you will be able to talk the language of library automation, make decisions, and move forward with a deeper knowledge of the impact of computers in all library operations and how to integrate technologies into library services."

Deborah Mazzolini, MLS
Library Director,
Belvedere-Tiburon Library,
Tiburon, California

CRC Press
Taylor & Francis Group
Boca Raton   London   New York

CRC Press is an imprint of the
Taylor & Francis Group, an **informa** business

Computers in Libraries
An Introduction for Library Technicians

THE HAWORTH INFORMATION PRESS®
Resources for Library Technicians
Mary L. Kao
Senior Editor

Computers in Libraries: An Introduction for Library Technicians
by Katie Wilson

Titles of Related Interest:

Cataloging and Classification for Library Technicians, Second Edition
by Mary L. Kao

Introduction to Serials Work for Library Technicians by Scott Millard

Introduction to Technical Services for Library Technicians
by Mary L. Kao

Computers in Libraries
An Introduction
for Library Technicians

Katie Wilson

CRC Press
Taylor & Francis Group
Boca Raton London New York

CRC Press is an imprint of the
Taylor & Francis Group, an **informa** business

Published by

The Haworth Information Press®, an imprint of The Haworth Press, Inc., 10 Alice Street, Binghamton, NY 13904-1580.

PUBLISHER'S NOTES
The development, preparation, and publication of this work has been undertaken with great care. However, the Publisher, employees, editors, and agents of The Haworth Press are not responsible for any errors contained herein or for consequences that may ensue from use of materials or information contained in this work. The Haworth Press is committed to the dissemination of ideas and information according to the highest standards of intellectual freedom and the free exchange of ideas. Statements made and opinions expressed in this publication do not necessarily reflect the views of the Publisher, Directors, management, or staff of The Haworth Press, Inc., or an endorsement by them.

Due to the ever-changing nature of the Internet, Web site names and address, though verified to the best of the publisher's ability, should not be accepted as accurate without independent verification.

Cover design by Christie R. Peterson.
TR: 9.25.06

Library of Congress Cataloging-in-Publication Data

Wilson, Katie.
    Computers in libraries : an introduction for library technicians / Katie Wilson.
       p. cm.
    Includes bibliographical references and index.
    ISBN-13: 978-0-7890-2150-2 (alk. paper)
    ISBN-10: 0-7890-2150-1 (alk. paper)
    ISBN-13: 978-0-7890-2151-9 (pbk. : alk. paper)
    ISBN-10: 0-7890-2151-X (pbk. : alk. paper)
    1. Libraries—Automation—Handbooks, manuals, etc. 2. Library science—Technological innovations—Handbooks, manuals, etc. 3. Library technicians—Effect of technological innovations on. I. Title.

Z678.9.W545 2006
025'.00285—dc22

                                     2005023843

For my father Phillip,
with all my love.
You passed on the words.

ABOUT THE AUTHOR

Katie Wilson, MLS (Grad Dip Lib), has worked in academic, public, and state libraries providing reference services, managing electronic research and digital and library systems. She established and managed a campus information technology training unit and has worked as a training consultant for a library software company. Katie pioneered the development of Web-based instructional material in several library environments, and enjoys teaching and writing about technology in libraries. She is currently managing digital and library systems at the State Library of New South Wales, Sydney, Australia.

CONTENTS

Preface and Acknowledgments

Computers and libraries are well suited, and libraries were early adopters of computer technology. The business of libraries is to collect and record information for access, and manage its shared use among a population base. The function of computers is to process representations of data and manage records.

This book discusses the use of computers in all library operations. It examines how the Internet has transformed and is challenging libraries. Before the Internet was popular libraries provided online database searching, an unfamiliar concept outside the library world. Now everyone knows and understands how to research a topic and find information on the Internet. However, data on the open World Wide Web have not undergone the quality control and selection processes used with library resources.

The challenge for libraries is to integrate unstructured information and emerging Internet technologies into the library collection.

During my research for this book I found *Library Automation for Library Technicians: An Introduction* (1986) by Joan Tracy, which made me aware of just how much the Internet has changed libraries. Libraries continue to be organized around functions such as acquisitions, cataloging, circulation, serials, and reference. Integrated library management systems still operate in modules based around library functionality. The difference between the 1986 publication and this book is the impact of the Internet on libraries. Internet technologies have moved library and information services into a digital age, challenging earlier practices and assumptions. Ordering and cataloging processes are streamlined and fast; reference and research services have turned into twenty-four hour help centers; and the library exists beyond a physical space. How will library technologies change in another twenty years?

The audience for this book is both practicing and new library technicians and library assistants. How have the roles of library technicians and assistants changed in the past twenty years? They are more involved in the practical, daily operations of library services, and that, as this book shows, encompasses computers, technology, and the Internet. The chapters of this book provide background and practical understanding of library system software, the Internet, information searching, the integration of digital and print collections, and issues of online access and authorization. One chapter is titled "The Internet in Libraries," but the Internet is discussed in every subsequent chapter because it is integrated into all library operations. The book's sub-subtitle could be *The Transformed Library and Information Workplace*.

I hope this book is read by people who want to find out about how computer technology operates in libraries and information centers, and what happens behind the library circulation desk or self-check machine.

I deeply thank Mary Kao for encouraging me to write this book. I have enjoyed researching, explaining, and gathering together the changing threads of computers in libraries. My friend Peggy Havukainen gave me the benefit of her knowledge and perspective as she read the chapters. I thank her immensely. Love to Vic Manuel, for his support and sustenance.

Chapter 1

Introduction to Computers

TERMINOLOGY

adaptive technology: Software and hardware used to adapt standard computers for individual needs.

ASCII (American Standard Code for Information Interchange): enables the exchange of data between different types of computers.

bus: Pathway for moving data in and out of a computer's central processing unit (CPU).

cache: A space used for temporary storage of data accessed by a computer.

card: A wired internal panel that contains memory and a chip that translates video and audio to a computer's monitor.

chip: A tiny calculator inside computer MICROPROCESSORS; also called a microchip.

client: A personal computer and software that interacts with a larger SERVER and its software.

CPU (central processing unit): or MICROPROCESSOR, the key part or brain of a computer.

data: Information input to a computer from a keyboard, an external device such as a DISK, or from another computer on a NETWORK.

disk: Storage devices such as a magnetic cylinder (hard disk), flat floppy disks, CD-ROMs, and DVDs.

(GUI) graphical user interface: Icons or images on a computer screen or monitor representing programs and files.

hardware: The physical pieces that make up a computer.

Internet: A worldwide NETWORK of networks.

(MHZ) megahertz: The speed of the microprocessor or CPU.

microprocessor: A computer's main calculating CHIP or central processing unit (CPU).

modem: The device that connects a computer to external networks via telephone or cable lines.

motherboard: The main circuitry board to which CHIPS and wires are attached.

MS DOS: One of the first Microsoft OPERATING SYSTEMS used in personal computers.

network: Computers connected by cables or remote sensing software within a house, an office, a building, or over a geographic area.

(NC or Net PC) network computer: A computer with a very small amount of memory connected to a larger computer via a network.

operating system: Software that enables the functionality and operations of a computer, e.g., Microsoft Windows for PCs, MAC OS (for Macintosh computers).

(PC) personal computer: Personal or small individual computer or workstation.

port: A slot or space on the outside of a computer to attach external devices such as printers, scanners, tape backup drives, removable CD-ROM or floppy-disk drives. See also USB.

RAM (random access memory): used for temporary storage of data for processing.

scanner: A device that reads data from a barcode and inputs it to the computer; also called a wand.

server: A mainframe or minicomputer that stores data and software and serves or distributes it to smaller CLIENT computers.

software: The programs, operating systems, and applications stored inside a computer.

supercomputer: A large, powerful computer capable of huge calculations.

thin client: Software that uses a small amount of memory, adapted for a NETWORK COMPUTER.

USB (universal serial bus): a port or plug opening that connects devices such as printers, disk drives, and memory cards to computers.

The idea of a computer, a machine that could make arithmetic calculations, had its origins over two centuries ago but at that time it was difficult and expensive to construct and did not come to fruition. In 1945 American scientist Vannevar Bush (Bush, 1945) wrote a now-famous article, "As We May Think," in which he previewed the idea of a computer, calling it a memex:

> A memex is a device in which an individual stores all his books, records, and communications, and which is mechanized so that it may be consulted with exceeding speed and flexibility. It is an enlarged intimate supplement to his memory. On the top are slanting translucent screens, on which material can be projected for convenient reading. There is a keyboard, and sets of buttons and levers. (p. 106)

This describes personal or desktop computers, but other types of computers also exist.

TYPES OF COMPUTERS

The first computers seem crude and unsophisticated now but at their beginnings they were a milestone, marking the start of the information revolution. Computers began to be manufactured in the early 1950s. The earliest were large mainframe computers with multiple cabinets to house the magnetic tapes used for storage. Each mainframe was located in a temperature-controlled room, had its own separate operating system, software and data-storage format, and could not exchange data with other computers. In 1963 the American Standard Code for Information Interchange, or ASCII, was developed to enable data to be shared between different computers. Mainframe computers were used for large calculations such as accounting, payroll, statistics, scientific research, banking, and stock control.

A minicomputer, a smaller, more compact version of a mainframe computer, used transistor circuits instead of vacuum tubes. Minicomputers generated so little heat that they did not need to be located in air-conditioned rooms, and became much more accessible to individuals. The minicomputer was the earliest version of what we now know as a personal computer (PC).

Two brands dominate the personal computer market. The IBM PC, developed in 1981, is made by a large number of companies and uses the graphical MS Windows operating system. The Macintosh personal computer, designed, developed, and made by Apple, Inc., has its own graphical operating system, MAC OS. PCs and Macintoshes are manufactured in two formats:

1. Desktop computers whose monitor, keyboard, CPU, and disk drives are separate physical pieces connected together.
2. Laptop or portable computers whose parts combine into one small physical unit, operating from battery as well as electrical power.

Servers are large-capacity computers that store and serve out software and data to smaller client personal computers. For example, a library integrated management system is stored on a server, and personal computers accessing it use client versions of the system software to interact with the server program.

A network computer (NC) is similar to a personal computer but it has a smaller hard disk with little memory for temporary storage. The NC connects to a server on a network and uses the server's hard disk to access software and store files. NCs' software is known as thin client because the programs are small and use less memory than regular

PCs with big hard disks (fat clients!). Most of the data processing occurs on the server. NCs require less maintenance and administration and are used in some business environments, and libraries or information centers for public access services. Sometimes called Net PCs, they access the Internet and can be adapted to access digital and cable television.

A supercomputer is a large and powerful number-crunching computer used by research and scientific organizations for large calculations of complex data. The most well-known supercomputer model is Cray.

HOW COMPUTERS WORK

A computer is made up of hardware and software. The hardware is anything physical—the casing, the boards containing wiring and chips, disk drives, etc. Software is what makes it all happen: the programs that operate a computer (operating systems such as Macintosh OS, Microsoft Windows, and Linux). Application programs on a computer, such as word processing, electronic mail, and integrated library management systems are also software.

A CPU or central processing unit microprocessor or chip (hardware) interprets and carries out instructions or commands from operating systems and application programs (software). Data are input to a computer via a keyboard, copied from a network or another disk and processed by the microprocessor. The same microprocessor outputs data, at a command, to the computer's monitor, printer, another computer on a network, or to a portable disk. A bus (USB) moves data in and out of the CPU. The measurement of CPU speed is in MIPs—million instructions per second. Although the CPU can work millions of instructions per second, it can only process one instruction at a time. To manage the time spent on each instruction, the CPU has a system clock that measures millions of cycles per second or megahertz (MHz); one million times per second equals 1 MHz. The type of chip often is incorporated into the name of a computer for example Intel Pentium chips.

Hardware

The storage box of a desktop computer is a square or rectangle casing that contains many of the operating hardware components. Figure 1.1 shows examples of hardware input and output components.

 Ports

Ports are openings to attach devices to a computer, for example, a printer, modem, mouse, and keyboard. At the back of a computer are a number of pins or holes with cables connected. Serial ports (nine pins) attach equipment such as network cables and external modems for external data connections (although more modems are internal). Parallel ports have twenty-five pins and faster transmission than serial ports for connecting devices such as printers, scanners, and tape backup units.

A USB (universal serial bus) is a faster port that enables the connection of many devices without special card adapters including portable disk drives, printers, scanners, memory sticks, and external hard drives. The keyboard and mouse connect through a circular PS/2 port and via a USB port.

Two different ports are used for communications or network connections. An Ethernet network cable plugs into the Ethernet port to provide local network and Internet connections, and a smaller port takes a phone cable to the modem for dial-up connection to the Internet.

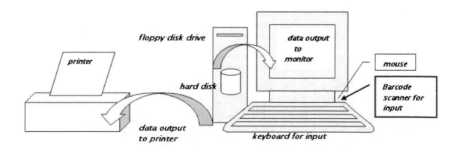

FIGURE 1.1. Hardware input and output components of a computer.

Cards are flat, electronically wired components that slot inside the computer's storage box, for example:

- Network cards enable connections to external networks.
- Graphics cards convert video data to display on the monitor.
- Sound cards enable a computer to interpret and deliver audio.

The motherboard is a circuitry board that contains the computer's chips and microprocessors, plug-in boards, and cards. A laptop computer does not have a separate storage box; instead, its components are miniaturized and stored internally beneath the keyboard.

Storage Devices

A computer has multiple disks and drives for storing and transferring data. A disk is hardware, and the data or programs stored on a disk are software, in the same way that a movie is data (software) on a DVD or video cassette (hardware).

A drive stores a disk that is either fixed (hard) or portable (floppy, zip, CD, DVD). The hard disk, made of aluminum and glass, is used for long-term storage of software applications or programs, data, and files. The size of a hard disk is measured in billions of bytes or gigabytes (GB), for example, a hard disk can measure 30 or 40 GB. A computer can have a partitioned (split) hard disk, labeled as C or D, or an external hard disk.

Portable disk drives are either built into the hardware or detachable. The smallest is the floppy-disk drive, labeled as A, with a storage capacity of about 1.44 megabyte (MB). A zip disk stores up to 100MB of data.

Larger capacity CD/DVD disk drives use many variations of optical disk technology (with acronyms) to store gigabytes of data, for example:

- CD-ROM (compact disc read-only memory) disks
- CD-R disks are CD-ROMs to which data can be copied only once

- Rewritable CD-RW/DVD disks write data, erase and rewrite, multiple times. CD-RW drives (known as CD burners) are good for storing or backing up data from a personal computer.
- DVD (digital video disc) is a type of CD that holds images, video, and text.

Memory sticks are small, thin, silicon plug-in components with different capacities used to store and transfer data, text, graphics, or digital images from one electronic device to another. For example, images move from a digital camera to a PC via a memory stick; e-mail can move between computers via a stick. Portable storage devices are changing continually, becoming more compact, larger in capacity, and more streamlined.

Large computers or servers such as those used to store library systems use an external magnetic tape drive for daily or regular backup of data or networked backup solutions for fast automatic backup from more than one computer.

Computers connected to a local network may show drives labeled as G, H, I, J, K, S, W, Z. These letters refer to network drives enable people in an organization to share data, and store backed up or copied data from a personal computer.

Monitor

The monitor is the screen that displays a computer's data. A monitor uses either cathode ray tube (CRT), or liquid crystal display (LCD) technology. LCD monitors are thin and flat, they flicker less, and are used in laptop computers as well as some personal computers, replacing CRT technology. CRT monitors are fatter, like a TV set.

Screen resolution refers to the pixels or dots that display an image on a monitor screen. For example, 1,024 × 768 means 1,024 pixels display on 768 lines. A pixel (short for picture element), is a single point in a graphic image. The higher the resolution (more pixels), the sharper the image. You can adjust the resolution from the Display Setting Properties in the Control Panel.

Peripherals

Hardware includes peripheral devices—equipment that attaches to a computer. Ports at the back or side connect devices such as a mouse, printer, plug-in disk drives, drawing tablets, digital cameras, personal digital assistants (PDAs), and fax machines. In libraries, barcode scanners, handheld and stationary, scan or read barcodes from patron cards and library items into the computer.

Memory

RAM is random access memory, which is used for temporary storage of data that the computer processes. A computer cannot use stored data directly so it copies data to the temporary RAM. For example, when editing a file, the computer creates a temporary copy of the file and stores it in the RAM for data manipulation. Saving a file writes it to the system's hard drive; the temporary copy of the file disappears after closing the file. If a file is not saved the changes are lost when the computer is turned off because all RAM is removed. RAM is measured in megabytes (MB), for example 256, 512 MB RAM. The greater amount of RAM a computer has, the more processing it can manage at once.

Cache is an intermediate storage area where the most recently accessed data are stored. When a program needs to access data, it first checks the cache to see if the data are there, thus saving time.

Networks

A network is a group of computers connected together by:

1. Cables or wiring in a physical building or room, or in a wider area by satellite, underground, and undersea cable
2. Network server operating system software that enables computers to communicate with one another and transmit data across the cables or wires
3. Network cards in computers, e.g., Ethernet
4. Wireless network remote sensing technology in a specified geographical area to pick up a signal from a computer, so that physical cabling between the computer and the network is not required

A local area network (LAN) covers a small geographic area, e.g., a building, an office, library, city, or university. A wide area network

(WAN) is a collection of LANs connected by powerful high-speed cables. The Internet is the largest of all—a worldwide network of networks. It consists of multiple LANs and WANs in almost every country in the world. Wireless technology provides flexibility in the workspace and public areas. Wireless computers can be moved around without needing to be attached to network points, and there is no ugly cabling. Chapter 2 discusses in detail the use of the Internet in libraries.

Software

Software refers to the applications or programs on a computer. A piece of software can be as small as a Web browser, a word processing program, or as large as an integrated library management system.

Operating Systems

The operating system (OS) software controls all hardware and software tasks. Every computer must have an operating system to run other programs. MS DOS was the original textual or command-driven operating system developed for personal computers. Apple developed the first graphical operating system, and Macintosh continues to use the same proprietary MAC OS, modified, developed, and enhanced regularly. Microsoft developed MS Windows as a graphical operating system for PCs for home, professional, and business users. Figure 1.2 shows details of a Windows operating system on a PC. Linux and UNIX are computer operating systems used with servers.

Application Programs

Sitting on top of the computer's operating system software are the application programs used to create, edit, and output data. Thousands of different software applications exist, from word processing and spreadsheet programs, to visual art software, Internet access programs such as Web browsers and e-mail, database programs and more. Any processing on a computer requires an application program.

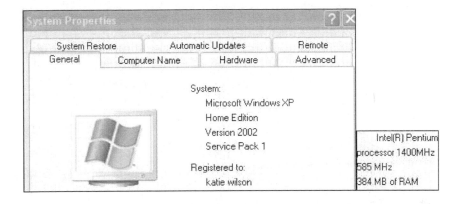

FIGURE 1.2. System properties window showing operating software, CPU processor, and RAM.

COMPUTERS IN LIBRARIES

The two types of computers found in libraries are servers and personal computers. A library's integrated management system is stored on a server. It may be located outside of the library in another building, for example, a specially designed and air-conditioned computer room. In a consortium, in which the system is shared among multiple member libraries, the server is stored in one location and accessed by member computers via a network.

Personal computers linked to the library system server via networks enable staff to carry out daily library transactions. The computers run client versions of the system software to search the catalog databases and access library records. This is known as a client-server relationship. Library patrons use personal computers to search the library's online catalog and the Internet, for word processing, and send e-mail. One personal computer can offer all of these activities, but many libraries separate them, limiting some computers to catalog searching only, others for e-mail or Internet research and word processing. Network computers, which have little local memory, provide Internet-only access in some public areas, and occasionally in staff workspaces.

Workstations

Personal computers sometimes are referred to as workstations. The term comes from the idea of a scholar's workstation, a PC with resources that a scholar or staff member uses in a work situation. For example, a cataloger's workstation may have access to the *Library of Congress Subject Headings* in electronic format, and MARC cataloging information, the library system cataloging module, and the Internet.

Adaptive Technology

Adaptive or assistive technology describes both hardware and software for use by people who have difficulties using standard computer setups. Some examples of adaptive technology in libraries are:

- keyboards with larger keys, those that use a wand or pen to touch the keys, or are onscreen
- large mouse trackballs that are easier to hold and move around, e.g., for children and elderly or disabled users
- voice output software that reads out data displaying on a screen
- voice recognition software that reads and inputs spoken data
- closed-circuit TV devices that magnify text
- Braille software and printers to create, edit, and output Braille documents.

REVIEW QUESTIONS

1. List five hardware components in a computer.
2. Define a graphical user interface.
3. Describe the difference between a Local Area Network (LAN) and a Wide Area Network (WAN).
4. Explain the client-server computer relationship.

Chapter 2

The Internet

TERMINOLOGY

asynchronous: Communication that takes place in different time frames, not at the same time, for example, E-MAIL.

bandwidth: The amount of data that can be sent over the Internet in a fixed amount of time.

blog (Web log, Weblog): A personal diary, travel guide or news resource on a Web site.

chat: Communication between people connected to the Internet, referred to as SYNCHRONOUS because it happens at the same time, in CHAT ROOMS; also called Internet Relay Chat (IRC).

chat rooms: Online virtual forums where people exchange information in real time on a range of topics using text messages. Some chat rooms incorporate graphics, audio, and video.

(e-mail) electronic mail: Communicating, sending messages and files to other computers across the Internet.

(FTP) file transfer protocol: Transferring files between computers across the Internet; used to download and upload files of catalog records between bibliographic networks, vendors, and library systems, and to transfer reports or data in and out of library systems.

firewall: Software that blocks access to and from servers to protect systems.

home page: A Web page for individuals or organizations.

HTML (hypertext markup language): The coding language that determines the display of data on the WORLD WIDE WEB.

HTTP (hypertext transfer protocol): The Internet standard that enables transmission of data across the WORLD WIDE WEB.

hypertext: The linking from words or images from one document to another; the basis of the WORLD WIDE WEB.

(IM) instant messaging: A communications service for creating on-line CHAT ROOMS.

Internet: A global computer network made up of smaller academic, government, educational, and commercial networks. Computers connect across the Internet using a common Internet protocol or language.

Internet Relay Chat (IRC): A method of synchronous communication in real time over the Internet in which groups of people or individuals discuss issues of interest. See also CHAT.

intranet: A Web site internal to an organization, limited to local access and contained within a FIREWALL.

IP address (Internet protocol address): A unique number that identifies a computer connected to the Internet, written in the format 123.234.23.1. The domain host name is the name equivalent of an IP address, written as your.library.org.

ISP (Internet service provider): A company or organization that provides access to the Internet.

LISTSERV: Internet software that creates MAILING or discussion lists.

mailing list: An Internet discussion group to which users subscribe via e-mail, send and receive messages from subscribed members of the group; uses the LISTSERV software.

newsgroup: Internet protocol for sharing information on a particular topic; also called Usenet newsgroups or NNTP (Network News Transfer Protocol).

protocol: A format for exchanging data between computers or devices.

RSS (Really Simple Syndication, Rich Site Summary, or RDF Site Summary): An Internet tool that creates feeds or updates from Web sites and alerts subscribers.

SMTP (Simple Mail Transfer Protocol): The Internet PROTOCOL used to send and receive e-mail.

SSH (Secure Shell): An Internet protocol and software program used to connect to, login, and access systems that provides more secure transmission of data than TELNET. SSH tunneling enables secure connections to other network ports and file transfer.

synchronous: Online communication that occurs at the same time, when sender and receiver respond simultaneously; see CHAT.

TCP/IP (Transmission Control Protocol/Internet Protocol): Formats for exchanging packets of data between computers on the Internet.

Telnet: A text only Internet protocol and software program for connecting to library catalogs and databases; largely replaced by the WORLD WIDE WEB but used for some internal system functions.

URL (uniform resource locator): A unique Internet address that identifies and locates a Web site; written in the format http://www.library.edu.

(www) World Wide Web: The Internet protocol that uses HYPERTEXT for linking Web sites.

Web site: Documents created for the World Wide Web using the coding program HTML (Hypertext Markup Language) incorporating text, images, animation, and video.

XML (eXtensible Markup Language): An extension of HTML used to describe the structure of digital objects and documents and enable sharing of data among different systems.

Z39.50: A communications standard that enables searching of online databases and catalogs through one interface. When Z39.50 is implemented on a library catalog system, you can search other databases using your own catalog search structure and interface.

The Internet is a global network that links multiple networks, and through them, millions of individual computers around the world. It developed from Advanced Research Projects Agency Network (ARPANET), a United States Department of Defense project in the late 1960s. Its revolutionary idea was the creation of network protocols or standards that use packet switching technology to enable the transfer of data between many networks, instead of having to connect through one central point. Research, scientific, and academic communities around the world adopted the Internet first, with commercial use beginning in the late 1990s. Its history is short but the impact of the Internet has been enormous. The development of computers and the Internet together produced the technological revolution of the late twentieth century. This chapter looks at some technical background to the Internet and its use in libraries.

INTERNET PROTOCOLS AND APPLICATIONS

The Internet uses specific protocols, rules, or standards for the exchange of data. The primary Internet technologies that control the transfer of data across networks are the combined packet switching protocols TCP/IP (Transmission Control Protocol and Internet Protocol). TCP breaks a document down into chunks or packets of data at their source, and reassembles the data at their destination. A document or file is sent in small bits so that it travels faster, and the receiver does not have to wait for the whole file to be delivered. The Internet protocol (IP) manages the delivery and addressing of the packets on the network. Every machine connected to the Internet has a unique IP address to identify its location. The IP address consists of four octets in binary format (eight digits), converted to decimals, e.g., 123.111.555.234. Each address has two parts, one to identify the network and the other to identify the host. The domain name is an alphabetical alias of the numeric address, for example, www.library.org. Internet protocols exist for specific functions and every activity on the Internet uses one of the protocols. E-mail uses SMTP, the Simple Mail Transfer Protocol. E-mail is sent and received between e-mail accounts. For example, the e-mail address <username@hostname. org> consists of a username and the name of the organization where the e-mail account is maintained. E-mail is asynchronous communication: messages are transmitted in different time frames. E-mail messages include the message text and attachments such as images or text files. Larger files such as software programs or files of bibliographic records are sent using the Internet file transfer protocol (FTP).

A mailing list is an Internet discussion group to which members subscribe, send, and receive messages via e-mail. Lists cover topics for people with a common interest. Software such as LISTSERV or Majordomo creates the mailing list and distributes e-mail to all subscribers. The software has specific instructions for joining and leaving a list. When you subscribe to a mailing list you receive copies of all messages sent to the group, including your own. People who subscribe to mailing lists and read, but do not send messages, are often called "lurkers." Thousands of different mailing lists exist on the Internet.

Internet chat services (also called Internet relay chat) use synchronous communication to interact with people at the same time. With chat services you can talk (with a microphone), send, receive, and respond to text messages instantaneously. As one participant types, the text displays on the other participant's monitor or computer screen. Chat sessions happen in chat rooms created with instant messaging (IM) software—virtual online spaces. Teleconferencing is Internet conferencing that uses chat, audio, video, and whiteboard, a shared space for writing online. Commercial software such as Microsoft's NetMeeting and WebEx allows participants to share software applications and see one another's computer desktops. Conferencing is used for online training, presentations, and demonstrations. These synchronous activities use the Session Initiation Protocol (SIP).

The Internet newsgroup protocol NNTP uses Usenet discussion group software to share and exchange information on a wide range of topics. A newsgroup is similar to a mailing list but you do not subscribe to a newsgroup. Instead, to view and send messages, you set up a connection to a newsgroup server, usually through an Internet service provider. Anyone can browse and read messages, as well as contribute to a newsgroup. Specific newsgroup software is needed for reading and sending news messages and is included in most Web browsers.

World Wide Web

The World Wide Web dominates the Internet because so much activity happens on the Web. However, it is only one of the Internet protocols. The Web was the invention of a software engineer named Tim Berners-Lee working at CERN, a high-energy physics laboratory in Switzerland in the late 1980s (Berners-Lee and Fischetti, 2000; Cailliau and Gillies, 2000). The idea grew out of a linking software program that Berners-Lee wrote to keep track of projects on his personal computer. Later, with the help of other CERN scientists, he extended the linking concept across the Internet and called it the World Wide Web. Its basis is hypertext, a format that enables the use of links (hyperlinks) to make references from one document to another document. The Web is not a database; it is a collection of documents stored on computers connected to the Internet. Users start at one Web page and follow its hypertext links to pages anywhere else.

Berners-Lee and the CERN team developed two standards for the Web:

1. HTML (hypertext markup language) is a coding scheme that determines the display of data in a Web document or file (Web page, home page, or Web site). HTML is a simplified version of SGML (standardized markup language), a markup scheme used in publishing.
2. HTTP (hypertext transfer protocol) enables the transfer of Web pages across the Internet. The prefix http:// is required at the beginning of every URL or Web address, for example <http://library.org>.

Physicists began using the Web to share research throughout the worldwide physics community. Soon after, other research and academic communities began developing Web servers, using server software to deliver Web pages to client computers.

To view material published on the World Wide Web your computer must have a Web browser. The browser receives, interprets, and displays HTML-encoded data from Web servers anywhere on the Internet. Students at the University of Illinois, Champaign-Urbana developed Mosaic, one of the first graphical Web browsers, and in 1994 Netscape Navigator grew out of Mosaic to become the first commercial Web browser. Until then, the Internet had been used only within the academic and research communities. Soon, the Internet opened up to the public and commercial markets. Many graphical Web browsers have developed, including Microsoft's Internet Explorer, Opera, and Mozilla Firefox.

The World Wide Web Consortium (W3C) a nonprofit organization located at MIT (Massachusetts Institute of Technology) and directed by Tim Berners-Lee, manages the technical standards and the development of the World Wide Web and HTML <http://w3c.org>.

The first library implementation of the Web was in 1991 at the Stanford Linear Accelerator Center (SLAC) in California, where Louise Addis, the librarian, saw the opportunity to link the library's online catalog with in-house documents in other formats. This application was true to the spirit of the Web that Tim Berners-Lee envisaged.

ACCESSING THE INTERNET

The Internet is a huge global network of networks, but how do you connect to it? To use the telephone you subscribe to a telecommunications provider. In the same way, an Internet service provider (ISP) provides access to the Internet. In your organization or library the Internet connection is available via a local network (LAN) within the building. Your organization arranges Internet access with an ISP, and the workplace is wired with network (Ethernet) cables that plug into your computer. When you turn on the computer, the network and Internet connections are active until you turn off the computer (or unplug the network cable). Your organization's information technology (IT) staff maintains the network and Internet access, user names, and passwords, e-mail addresses, and software on your computer.

Organizations use firewall software to protect networks and servers from unauthorized access or hacking.

To use the Internet at home or in a business, you need an ISP. For a monthly fee, the service provider gives you a username, password, and phone number. A cable connects the modem in your computer to your phone line, allowing you to dial up the Internet via telephone lines. Broadband services such as DSL (digital subscriber lines), ADSL (asymmetric digital subscriber lines), ISDN (integrated services digital network), or television cable modems provide faster access than the standard phone line. The term bandwidth refers to the amount of data that can be transmitted across cables or connections in a fixed amount of time. The greater bandwidth you have, the faster you can access the Internet.

 ## THE INTERNET IN LIBRARIES

When the Internet became widely available in the early 1990s, libraries were already using computers for many daily activities. Integrated library systems managed functions such as circulation, cataloging, and acquisitions. Computers and terminals provided public access to catalogs. Public services used dialup online and CD-ROM databases for reference and research. The Internet enhances library services and operations, improving communication and the transfer of data and it impacts on workflow and collections. Public and technical services use the Internet to search catalogs and databases, order library materials, transfer or download files of bibliographic records into catalogs, expand research options, and communicate with library users and staff. Libraries also establish intranets, internal Web sites for staff resources and information.

Integrated library systems provide a World Wide Web interface to the public catalog, the Web OPAC. The library catalog has become more than just a record of a library's collection. A library Web site includes links to other online catalogs and electronic databases, electronic journals, and Web sites selected by library staff. The Internet has raised the need for new and additional policies, and it is changing our expectations and use of information.

Public Services

Public services departments use library Web sites to provide information such as library hours, policies, address, events, and to publicize services to the community, for example in Figure 2.1. See Chapters 8 and 11 for further information about using HTML to create Web pages.

Reference Services

Reference services use the Web to provide research information for library users. Hypertext links on library Web pages lead to Internet material such as:

- government documents, newspapers, electronic journals, business and financial data;
- subject-based Web sites;
- directories such as the Librarians' Internet Index <http://www.lii.org>; and
- Web search engines.

Library patrons can search online subject database services and electronic journals from the Web OPAC. Patrons must be registered to use some services licensed to libraries. Chapter 10 discusses using databases and the Internet.

Online Reference

Web-based online reference services combine e-mail with Internet chat, inviting users to submit questions and interact with library staff in real time. Library staff answer questions, guiding users to relevant Web sites. After the session, users can receive, via e-mail, a complete transcript of the chat session, including links to web sites visited. *AskNow* <http://www.asknow.org/> is a free online reference service offered by libraries in countries such as the United States, Australia, and the Netherlands. The online reference service, *Ask a Librarian* from the Library of Congress, is shown in Figure 2.2 Some services use library staff in different time zones to answer questions, offering a twenty-four hour service.

FIGURE 2.1. Alameda County Library Web page showing community information and a link to search the catalog. Reprinted with permission.

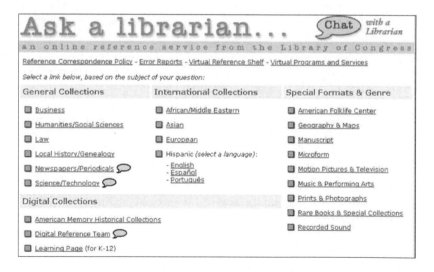

FIGURE 2.2. Ask a librarian, the Library of Congress's online reference service.

For a full list of online reference services in libraries, see the LiveRef(sm): A Registry of Real-Time Digital Reference Services at <http://www.public.iastate.edu/~CYBERSTACKS/LiveRef.htm>.

Security and Privacy

Libraries provide computers for Internet use, either free or for a fee, for patrons to research, check worldwide news, stock reports, sports scores, and use e-mail. This service is often accompanied by training in searching the Web, and using e-mail.

Use of the Internet in public areas in libraries has produced a set of issues and policy considerations. Before the Internet, libraries selected all materials for the collection, choosing not to purchase or accept offensive, inappropriate items. The Internet adds a wealth of useful information and research to library resources, but also includes data considered offensive or dangerous by some library users and staff.

Policies and procedures have been developed by libraries relating to Internet access and use. Some examples are:

- Filtering software installed on PCs or servers in public libraries blocks material considered unsuitable for children or offensive to some adult patrons and staff. The software prevents access to a set of Web sites and URLs, or restricts the display of Web sites containing undesirable words. Such action is in response to community pressure and legal action, although there has been parallel legal action against such practices.
- Internet acceptable-use policies that specify restrictions on certain Internet material, activities within the library, and staff use.
- Limited use of the Internet, e-mail, and chat on public computers because it inhibits access to core library use such as searching the catalog and researching on the Web.
- Implementation of restrictions on the use of the Internet for access to pornography.

Technical Services

The Internet forms the backbone of many tasks in library technical services. Acquisitions staff use the Internet to transmit electronic orders, claims, and cancellations from the library's integrated system to vendors. Electronic bibliographic records transfer into library catalog databases from bibliographic utilities in different instances:

1. When ordering library materials, bibliographic and order records download into the catalog from the acquisitions vendors.
2. Full bibliographic records download from a bibliographic utility.
3. New authority records purchased from a vendor or utility transfer into the catalog.

The transfer or downloading of records from the vendors or utility software uses one of two methods:

1. As a batch file, i.e., a file of multiple records, using the Internet file transfer protocol (FTP).
2. One record at a time, using FTP or the Z39.50 protocol.

Cataloging staff use the Internet as a resource for cataloging tools and support, such as the Library of Congress cataloging resources at <http://www.loc.gov>. E-mail and e-mail discussion lists allow catalogers to share experiences and problems. Cataloging staff apply skills and knowledge to the organizing and classifying of Internet resources.

Collection Development

The Internet is a powerful selection tool for collection development. Web-based library catalogs are a rich resource for material as are vendor and publisher Web sites. E-mail discussion lists provide forums for sharing information about selection and materials.

Internet and Web-based materials form a growing part of library collections. Libraries purchase access to electronic journals, newspapers, full-text articles, and electronic books published independently on the Web or through aggregators or distributors such as Academic Press, NetLibrary, Online Computer Library Center (OCLC), Project Muse, and JSTOR. For lists of electronic journals search the Librarians Internet Index <http://www.lii.org>.

Communication

In libraries and information centers e-mail is a primary means of communication internally with staff, and externally with patrons, vendors, bibliographic utilities, and other library suppliers. Integrated library systems send circulation notices (overdue, fines, bills, and hold pickups) via electronic mail.

The library community uses e-mail discussion groups or mailing lists to share and exchange information on a range of topics. Some examples are Web4Lib Electronic Discussion and Archives, which is a discussion on libraries and the World Wide Web, and PUBLIB and PUBLIB-NET, which are discussion groups for public libraries.

A blog (Web log or Weblog) is a Web site where people publish their own opinions, experiences, or selected resources for anyone else to read, similar to a personal newsgroup or diary. Group blogs share thoughts and activities within a family, community, or workgroup. Libraries and other organizations and use blogs as internal and external bulletin boards. Free blog software is available via sites such as blogger.com. Examples of library blogs are at Library Weblogs <http://www.libdex.com/weblogs.html> or Peter Scott's Library Blog at <http://blog.xrefer.com/>.

RSS (Really Simple Syndication, Rich Site Summary, or RDF Site Summary) is a tool for receiving updates and news or information from Web sites of your choice. RSS uses reader software called aggregators to collect and deliver the feeds to the computer as headlines and abstracts. Aggregators are client software, or Web-based tools, such as the free Bloglines RSS aggregator <http://www.bloglines.com>. Bloglines store RSS feeds for any Web site, as well as blogs. Figure 2.3 shows an example of a RSS reader.

When you sign up with an aggregator you nominate the RSS feeds or updates you wish to receive. RSS feeds are written in XML and display on a Web site with a link *Syndicate this site,* or a small XML icon. Click on the icon, or copy the URL link and paste it into the RSS aggregator software or Web site. For example, the Librarians' Internet Index <http://lii.org>, a regularly updated collection of reference material on the Web, provides RSS feeds. Some aggregators have alert options to notify users of updated RSS feeds.

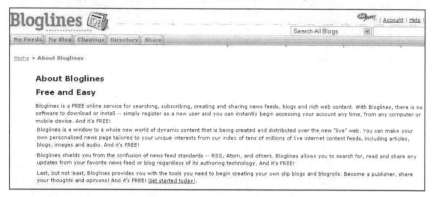

FIGURE 2.3. Bloglines, a Web-based RSS aggregator or reader. http://www.
bloglines.com/about/. Reprinted with permission.

As the Internet continues to expand, libraries contribute to its growth, and use it to extend their services. The following chapters in this book further explore the use of the Internet in libraries.

REVIEW QUESTIONS

1. What is the difference between synchronous and asynchronous communication on the Internet?
2. List four ways that the Internet is used in libraries and information centers.
3. What is the name of the unique number that every computer connected to the Internet must have?
4. How would you use a blog?

Chapter 3

Integrated Library Management Systems

TERMINOLOGY .

backup: Procedure for copying a library system database and transactions.

bibliographic record: Description of material provided by a library; includes title, author, subject, publication details.

bibliographic utility: An organization that provides bibliographic records to subscribing libraries; nonprofit organizations include Online Computer Library Center (OCLC), RLG (Research Libraries Group), or national such as the British Library National Bibliographic Service (NBS).

fixed field: A record field containing data that are fixed in length, e.g., codes, dates.

Integrated library management system (ILMS, ILS or LMS): Software that manages library operations with separate modules that interact and share a central database of records.

MARC (MAchine Readable Cataloging): An international standard for computerized bibliographic data, originally developed by the United States Library of Congress.

(NC) network computers: Computers with small hard drives that use THIN CLIENT technology to store and process software on a central server.

OPAC or PAC (Online Public Access Catalog): The public search interface to a library catalog.

open source software: Software that is freely available for people to use and develop.

(RDBMS) relational database management system: Database structure of integrated library systems; uses related data tables that interact to display information in response to searches.

Single function system: A library system that consists of only one module, e.g., circulation, acquisitions, serials, or cataloging.

software only system: An INTEGRATED LIBRARY MANAGEMENT SYSTEM in which only software is supplied by the vendors; the library purchases the hardware separately.

thin clients: Software and data stored and processed on a central server and delivered to NETWORK COMPUTERS.

turnkey system: INTEGRATED LIBRARY MANAGEMENT SYSTEM in which hardware comes with installed software and the library simply has to "turn on the key" to start the system.

variable-length field: A bibliographic record field containing data of any length, either free text or in a specific format such as MARC.

The first library management software was developed in the late 1970s and 1980s to automate library card catalogs and circulation processes. These homegrown products were usually separate, stand-alone programs that later became commercial, expanding to include modules representing multiple library processes. The modules are integrated, and interoperate, linking to a central database of records. Vendors of integrated library systems have close interactions with their user groups, developing and customizing their systems to meet client needs.

A computer is defined as a device that *processes representations* in a *systematic way* (Crane, 2003). Integrated library management systems store *representations* of library material as catalog records, and the people who use and access the material as patron records. The*systematic processes* include the acquiring, cataloging and circulation of material, and its display in the Online Public Access Catalog (OPAC). This chapter looks at the structure, administration, and management of integrated library systems. Although not all modules discussed are found in every library system, the processes and work-flows used by systems are similar.

SYSTEM STRUCTURE

An integrated library management system (ILMS) contains modules that represent all recordable library operations. The modules are linked, and all share and have access to the central database of library records, the catalog. The primary functions are: ordering and receiving material, recording financial or accounting data, describing the collection, and recording the borrowing and use of material within a library. The system manages the input and output of data (creating and editing records), and the storage and manipulation of data (circulation and acquisitions transactions).The catalog represents more than just the material within a library's physical structure. Using the Internet, library systems link to electronic books, electronic journals, full-text databases, and virtual or digital libraries. For example, The Los Alamos National Laboratory Library Without Walls builds collections of publications and research in digital format with electronic finding tools: <http://library.lanl.gov/lww.html>.

Most library users see only the online catalog and circulation modules of a library system, and are unaware of the automated tasks involved in stocking, running, and maintaining a library. Systems are, of course, much more complex than they seem from the outside. An integrated library system manages library operations within the following separate modules:

- *Acquisitions:* select, order, budget, receive, pay for material; claim and cancel late orders or those not received
- *Cataloging:* create records, describe, classify, and annotate with local data
- *Serials:* describe and check-in serial issues, route to staff or patrons, record binding and claim late issues
- *Circulation:* record circulation of material to patrons in and out of the library

- *Interlibrary Loans:* lend and borrow material from other libraries
- *OPAC (Online Public Access Catalog):* display library resources to patrons

The only tasks not part of an integrated system are physical ones such as shelving, repair, and binding. However, the system can indicate when items undergo one of these activities.

System Software

Integrated library systems are packaged and sold as turnkey, software-only, or single-function systems. With a turnkey system a library purchases the acquisitions, cataloging, circulation, OPAC, serials control, and other modules, as well as hardware, installation, staff training, ongoing maintenance and technical support, troubleshooting, and software upgrades. A software-only system includes the same software and training components as the turnkey system, without the hardware and hardware maintenance. The library purchases hardware separately, according to the system vendor's requirements. A library may purchase a single-function system for just one application such as circulation, acquisitions, serials, or cataloging. In addition, integrated library system vendors offer individual modules for purchase, and stand-alone software products such as resource linking and federated searching supplements and integrate with other systems. Over 100 commercial library management system vendors operate globally. Their products range from large integrated systems that combine multiple modules to small systems that include only core modules such as cataloging and circulation. Library Technology Guides <http://www.librarytechnology.org/> lists library system vendors, libraries worldwide by type, and trends and developments in the field of library automation. Libdex, the Library Index <http://www.libdex.com/vendor.html> lists library system vendors and the libraries that use their products, as well as a geographic listing of libraries with automated library systems.

Open-source library system software is freely available for use and adaptation as an alternative to vendor, that is, "proprietary" library software. Koha <http://www.koha.org/> is an example of an open-source integrated library system: one organization developed its source code, and its creators and volunteers around the world maintain and develop the software. The Georgia Library PINES program is developing an open source integrated library system called Evergreen for a consortium of over 250 public libraries in the state of Georgia. <http://www.open-ils.org/>. Greenstone Digital Library Software <http://www.greenstone.org/> is open-source software for building and distributing digital library collections, as well as publishing on the Internet or on CD-ROM. Both products are offered freely or for a small fee under the GNU General Public License.

Databases and Record Types

A library system has two primary databases:

1. The bibliographic database stores records of material provided by a library. Within the database are the following record types:
   - bibliographic records describing each title or piece of information in the library catalog
   - authority records providing references or links from alternative names, subjects, and titles
   - order records tracking material being acquired
   - item or holding records identifying each copy a library holds
   - serial checkin records and cards tracking receipt of individual serial issues.
2. The patron database records users of the library system:
   - patron records identify each borrower or user, interact with item records, and store statistics
   - item records interact with patron records, storing the date checked out, and date due for each circulation

Figure 3.1 shows the interaction of record types in the library system.

A bibliographic record originates when staff orders a title. Item records link to the bibliographic record for each copy of a title received and for as long as the item remains in the library system.

In an integrated system, all modules can access the bibliographic records. Transactions such as editing a record, or a circulation action on a record, are dynamic—the change takes place immediately, and the updated record is seen from all modules.

Most integrated library systems use a relational database management system (RDBMS) made up of tables, rows, and columns containing elements from bibliographic, item or holding, order, serial, and patron records. If data from a record change one table, they

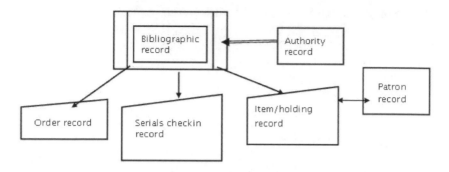

FIGURE 3.1. Interaction of library system records.

change in all related tables. Data from different system tables combine for output in answer to a query or search. For example, bibliographic and item data display in the online public catalog; overdue notices include data from bibliographic, item, and circulation tables; data from order, vendor or supplier, and bibliographic tables combine to display material on order in the OPAC (Large, Tedd, Hartley, 1999).

Data are stored in records in two formats:

1. *fixed fields:* contain fixed-length data such as dates, and codes stored in system data tables, e.g., vendors and fund codes in order records
2. *variable-length fields:* contain data in a specific format, for example, bibliographic titles, authors, patron names, or free text for internal processing notes.

 SYSTEM ADMINISTRATION

The local management of an integrated library system is known as system administration. Tasks include managing the hardware, internal and external access to the system, security, backing up the databases and daily transactions on a regular basis, troubleshooting, performing system upgrades, and communicating with the vendor support staff. The system administrator monitors performance of the system, and checks on usage of allocated disk space, record numbers, and licensed users. Several staff members may share this job, or it may be the responsibility of one person. Cooperation with local information technology staff is essential.

Hardware and Software

An integrated library system consists of a number of hardware and software components. The system server contains:

- Server operating software
- Proprietary system client and server software written for Linux, Java, and Windows operating systems (owned by the vendor or company), or freely available, open-source software.

Disk drives with large storage capacities (many gigabytes) contain:

- Catalog and patron databases
- Image or digital databases
- Local databases such as newspaper indexing, community information, and archives

Backup

A backup procedure regularly copies or backs up the system databases and daily transactions including circulation activity, database additions, and updates. The system administrator schedules regular, daily backups, using high-capacity tapes, to run automatically at a scheduled time or manually as required, preferably at a low-usage time. The backup process uses a set of tapes for every day of the week, with tapes stored off site for security and safety purposes. Centralized automated backup methods use separate third-party software such as Legato or Veritas.

The system administrator ensures that the system hardware is always powered up or turned on. System servers use a separate, uninterruptible power supply (UPS) to provide several minutes of emergency additional power and allow for the orderly shutdown of hardware components if accidents occur and the power supply is disconnected during storms, hurricanes, cyclones, floods, or power outages.

Access to Systems

Access to the library system server is available from client personal computers. The server and client personal computers both connect to a local area network (LAN) that is part of an organizational, regional, state, or national network connected to the Internet. The server connects permanently to the local network via a network cable, and client computers connect with network cables or wireless network remote-sensing technology. The server and client computers do not have to connect to the same local area network; both have in common an Internet connection that enables access from anywhere in the world. Figure 3.2 shows the relationship between client computers and the library system server. An organization's information technology staff maintains network access and connections in conjunction with the library system administrator.

The server computer uses a server version of the system software. Client computers use a client version of the system software to access staff system modules, and client Web browser software to view the Web OPAC. Public computers require only client Web browser software.

An alternative method for connecting computers to the system server uses thin client technologies for staff and public access. Network PCs, personal computers with small local hard disks and limited memory, connect via a local network to an intermediary server that stores all software applications and temporary file space. Data processing does not occur at the network PC but at the terminal server, from where it passes to the library system server.

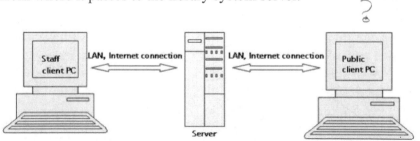

FIGURE 3.2. Client, network, and server connections.

Library staff use client computers to create and edit catalog records, search the catalog database, and process loans. Patrons search the catalog from computers and portable devices both inside and outside the library, from home, work, or dormitories. Staff and public users have a different view of the bibliographic and patron records. The staff view shows full bibliographic records, and linked order, item, and serial records. The public view is briefer and includes availability status or due date combined with selected bibliographic data and call number. The labels or descriptions of data fields are less technical than MARC bibliographic field labels. For example, *imprint* converts to *publisher* in the public record view. Libraries can customize the format and labeling of records for the OPAC.

Authorization

For security reasons, staff members require authorization to access the library system. This is to protect data stored on the system server, to maintain the integrity of the bibliographic data, and to preserve the privacy of patron data. Managing the authorization of users is a system administration task, with up to two levels of authorization:

1. Login management provides security and controls who can access the system.
2. Functional authorization controls the functionality on the system, and is allocated to staff according to skills and work requirements.

The system records all logins, enabling a System Administrator to track system usage and produce statistical reports.

Most library catalogs are available to the public both locally and via the Internet; public users do not require authorization. Exceptions are:

- government or private organizations that do not provide public access to their catalogs for security reasons
- patrons viewing their personal records through the online public access catalog are required to provide authentication details
- searching commercial databases licensed to libraries from library catalogs requires patron authentication

MANAGEMENT
AND STATISTICAL INFORMATION

All library system modules incorporate policies that library managers review and update throughout the life of the system. Managers can obtain information about how each system module functions on a daily basis, who the users are, and other valuable reporting and statistical data.

Statistics, Reports, and Coding

A key function of an integrated library system is its ability to gather and report information and statistics on the activities of the system. Some examples are:

- daily circulation statistics
- financial reports
- material cost projections
- record counts
- bibliographies by title, subject, author
- lists of records based on criteria such as location and types of material
- groups of patrons measuring numbers of loans
- cross-tabulation of statistics such as types of patrons, and types and numbers of loans

ILMS can generate standard, predefined reports, and customized reports according to a library's statistical and reporting needs. Staff can download or output reports to third-party software packages such as spreadsheets, reference management programs, and databases for further manipulation.

However, a system's reporting functions are only as good as the data recorded within it. Libraries may have specific reporting needs, but if the required data are not stored in the records, they cannot be extracted for reports. For example, a library may need to report on the language background of patrons. This requires that every patron record include their primary language. To make it easier for library staff to record language during patron registration, a fixed field in the patron record can be labeled Language. A list of languages spoken in the community, with corresponding codes, is created and stored in a table. To generate statistical reports, the library staff uses the system's reporting capability to gather and count the language values from all patron records.

The successful gathering of useful statistical reports, then, depends on these key factors:

1. Analysis of the library's statistical needs at system installation, with regular review and revision as needs change.
2. Coding of data to be reported on.
3. Storage of coded statistical data in the system.
4. Accurate use of codes by staff when creating records.

Bibliographic records include codes that indicate the format of material (e.g., book, video, journal, electronic resource, microfiche, or thesis). Library staff create reports on material formats combined with other values such as location to create more complex reports. Patrons use the same codes to refine and limit catalog searches in the OPAC. Figure 3.3 shows limit options for an OPAC search using location, type of item, or language data from bibliographic records.

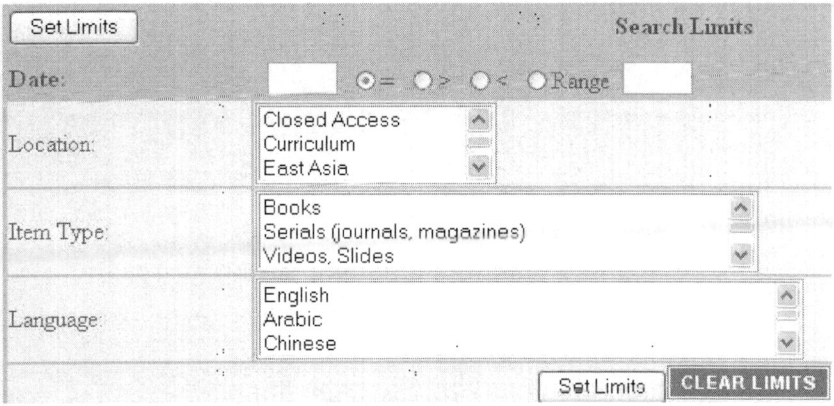

FIGURE 3.3. Example of OPAC search limits based on bibliographic record values.

Patron Search Statistics

The library system stores details of patron searches from the public catalog. Search analysis shows the following:

- the indexes searched (author, title, subject, keyword);
- the actual words searched;
- subsequent actions, for example, selecting a specific record from a result list, or following a system suggestion to view a related term or heading; and
- searches refined or limited.

Search statistics provide information on how patrons search, and where searches are unsuccessful. Library staff can use search reports to develop help screens and bibliographic instruction for patrons and to order material on topics patrons are seeking.

The following chapters examine in more detail the use of integrated library systems within different library operations.

REVIEW QUESTIONS

1. How does a turnkey library management system differ from a software-only system?
2. Name two key system administration tasks.
3. Name two possible methods or levels of authorization of users of a library system.
4. What are two types of search statistics a library system may report on?

Chapter 4

Acquisitions

acquisitions: The integrated library system module for creating and maintaining orders for material; includes a financial management section.

appropriation: A financial amount allocated to library funds, usually on an annual basis.

approval plan: An agreement between a library and a VENDOR by which the latter sends new material on an approval basis; items can be returned by the library if not approved.

bibliographic utility: An organization that sells and distributes MARC bibliographic records.

bibliographic verification: The researching of bibliographic details to correctly identify an item to order.

BISAC (Book Industry Standards and Communications): A U.S. based group that maintains standards for the electronic data interchange ordering formats for books and serials; *see also* EDIFACT.

blanket order: An agreement between a library and a VENDOR whereby the library accepts all titles sent by a vendor according to profiles defined by the library; items cannot be returned.

cancellation: Communication from a library to a vendor that an item that is no longer needed or from a VENDOR to a library that an item is not available for purchase.

cash balance: The fund balance available for spending, including encumbered amounts.

claim: A request sent to a VENDOR for an item that has not been received.

collection development: Policies set by a library that define the nature of its collection, to meet the readership and functional needs of the library.

e-book: An electronic book whose whole content is digital, which is downloaded to a local computer or other portable device for viewing and reading.

e-journal: An electronic journal with completely digitized text and images accessible via the Internet through library subscriptions, or for free.

EDIFACT (Electronic Data Interchange for Administration, Commerce and Transport): An international standard for online or electronic ordering using file transfer protocol (FTP). *See also* BISAC.

encumbrance: The estimated price committed to a fund at the point of ordering.

expenditure: The amount actually paid for items and charged to a fund; may be more or less than the amount encumbered.

firm order: An order for a MONOGRAPH item that is not part of an APPROVAL PLAN or STANDING ORDER subscription.

fiscal close: The closing of funds at the end of a fiscal or financial year.

free balance: The fund balance available after payments, not including encumbrances.

ISBN (International Standard Book Number): a unique number allocated to each monograph published; used by publishers and libraries to identify publications.

ISSN (International Standard Serial Number): a unique number allocated to SERIALS by publishers; used to identify serial publications.

journal aggregators: Companies that license full-text journal material from multiple sources and package it into one online source for distribution.

MARC (MAchine Readable Cataloging): An international standard for computerized bibliographic data, originally developed by the United States Library of Congress.

monograph: A non-SERIAL publication that is a single or multivolume, e.g., book, encyclopedia.

out-of-print: Items no longer printed by publishers; some VENDORS specialize in obtaining out-of-print material.

(PO) purchase order: An order for material with a unique number assigned to each order.

SAN (Standard Address Number): A unique number used with electronic ordering to identify VENDORS and libraries.

serial: A publication in successive parts issued at regular or irregular intervals, e.g., journal, newspaper, newsletter, yearbook, annual report, periodical.

shopping cart, basket: Options on VENDOR Web sites to place orders for library material.

standing order: A monograph order that continues to be supplied by a VENDOR as it is published.

vendor: A seller and distributor of material for library collections; also known as a jobber, book dealer, or subscription agent (for serials).

Z39.50: A communication protocol that enables seamless searching connection from one library system to other catalogs, databases.

A library collection begins with acquisitions, and almost every step in this process involves the use of computers. The integrated library system acquisitions module manages the ordering of material, payment, and tracking of orders. Collections include digitized maps, images, scientific data, research, online databases, electronic books and journals, as well as hard-copy material within library buildings. Library users download electronic books and journals or read them online. Electronic communication enables the transmission of paperless orders between library systems, vendors, and online bookstores. This chapter looks at the use of computers in the acquisitions workflow.

ACQUISITIONS PROCESS

Acquiring material for a library starts with the intellectual and professional selection process. Requests for items come from a number of sources:

- the library's collection development policy and procedures;
- library users or patrons; and
- the requirements for teaching programs in educational institutions.

Acquisitions staff can create or download bibliographic and order records. The library catalog database stores the records and staff can follow the progress of orders, claiming or canceling late items, and editing records to reflect any changes. When the library receives an item its receipt date and payment status are recorded, and the staff processes it for the library's collection.

Parallel to the ordering process, an acquisitions module may contain a financial accounting component that tracks the allocation of library funds, the encumbrance and expenditure or payment of material. As the system receives an order it encumbers or commits a monetary amount against a fund, reducing the cash balance—the amount available for spending. When the item arrives in the library the system charges the price paid to the fund, reducing the free balance—funds available for spending excluding encumbrances.

Vendors

An acquisitions vendor is an organization or company that supplies material to libraries. Libraries use multiple vendors according to the nature of collections. For example, some vendors include:

- online bookstores
- chain, and local independent bookstores
- university bookstores
- publishers and university presses
- associations or organizations such as library associations, scientific associations
- out-of-print specialists
- government departments
- video and audio distributors
- distributors or aggregators of serials, electronic journals, books, and databases
- citation database producers

Serials vendors are subscription agents that arrange and renew bulk subscriptions and supply consolidated invoices. Book or monograph vendors provide electronic bibliographic records, approval plans, and shelf-ready cataloged and bar-coded library material. All vendors have Web sites and many offer online ordering. A useful source of acquisitions vendors is the AcqWeb Directory of Publishers and Vendors at <http://acqweb.library.vanderbilt.edu/acqs/.html>.

Vendor Records

Acquisitions personnel create and maintain vendor records in the acquisitions module, storing postal address, phone and e-mail address, and library account numbers for each vendor. If vendors use electronic ordering, the SAN (Standard Address Number), a seven-digit identifier for both vendors and the library, is stored to ensure unique identification. The SAN prevents billing errors, books being shipped to the wrong places, and errors in payments and returns. The *American Library Directory* lists library SANs. The Bowker directory *Books In Print* lists and regularly updates vendor SANs.

When creating an order record acquisitions staff can select a vendor and insert the vendor code into the order record. The vendor and order records are linked allowing staff to view the vendor record from within an order record. The library system gathers and stores vendor statistics for reporting purposes, including number of items ordered, received, claimed and canceled, the monetary amounts spent, and delivery times.

Approval Plans

Libraries use approval plans and blanket orders as part of their collection development procedures. Under these arrangements vendors supply library material using customized library profiles based on subject, geography, or readership. For example, a profile could include:

- all Latin American publications
- selected art or music titles
- titles from specified publishers

Vendors use approval plans to send libraries selected titles based on profiles. The library reviews titles and returns those not approved or those that do not fit the collection profile. Under blanket orders vendors supply all titles that fall within a particular subject or geographic profile, and libraries accept them without review. Advantages of approval plans and blanket orders include price discounts and the prompt delivery of material because vendors can prepare the orders in advance.

An electronic approval plan allows the library system to interact with the vendor's system. Staff can download files of MARC bibliographic records using file transfer protocol (FTP). As the data download, the system checks for duplicate titles, series, and ISBNs and notifies staff of possible duplicates already in the catalog. Staff members review the titles and reject or approve them, generating order records and fund encumbrances for approved titles. The system adds accepted orders to invoices for payment using electronic processing. The status of order records changes to indicate their status for rejected titles. A file of rejected orders can be sent back to the vendor and deleted from the catalog if necessary.

Library Material

Libraries collect a wide range of material in many different formats. In addition to traditional print books, journals, and magazines, new electronic formats have emerged. When collecting nonprint material correct devices and methods must be available to access the material. For example, material formatted onto CD-ROMs needs to be read or viewed on computers with CD-ROM drives. Audio and music CDs and movies in video and DVD (digital video disc) formats need specific equipment to be played, listened to, or watched.

Electronic Books

An e-book or electronic book is a digitized book reproduced from a book in print (on paper) or it may begin its life digitally. E-books include both fiction and textbook titles. Generally, the e-book layout mirrors a print book with title and table of contents pages, chapters, and indexes. The market for e-books has developed slowly. Takeovers and buyouts have occurred as vendors struggle to establish the concept of reading books digitally and develop the technology. A variety of software is in use and several standards exist for e-book file formats. Some e-book companies have adapted existing software such as Adobe Reader; others offer their own e-book reader software. International Digital Publishing Forum <www.idpf.org> is an international trade and standards organization that develops specifications and standards for the electronic publishing industry.

Licensing choices range from selecting titles from different vendors to offering whole databases of e-books. Options for accessing e-books (Lee, 2002) include:

- view and browse directly online via the Internet
- download into portable e-book readers (some libraries lend e-book readers to patrons)
- download to computers and PDAs (personal digital assistants) with e-book reading software installed
- print on demand from e-book companies or libraries

For example, NetLibrary, ebrary Inc., and OverDrive are suppliers of e-books. After going through a secure authentication process registered patrons access the e-books from hypertext links in online catalogs. Patrons can browse e-books online for any length of time, print pages, or "check out" a book, a process in which the book is assigned to a computer using an encrypted signature. During this time the e-book may not be used by another reader. Checkout time periods are set by the library and range from hours to days. Figure 4.1 shows a bibliographic record for a NetLibrary item.

For libraries that offer e-books from a range of vendors and for different devices the online catalog will have multiple software download links for computers, PDAs, and vendor-specific reader software.

Electronic Journals

The adoption of electronic journals (e-journals) has progressed more quickly than e-books, and a large number of journals are available only in electronic format. E-journals are accessible via the Internet using a variety of formats and payment models:

- as a print subscription as well as electronically, sometimes with a discount for the purchase of both formats
- available only electronically
- freely available
- made available by publishers through e-journal aggregators
- accessed from a preprint archive or an individual's Web site
- some are peer-reviewed or refereed

Libraries have to provide software, hardware, adequate Internet access, and maintain secure systems to authorize patrons for electronic books and journals.

Education and technology [electronic resource] : an encyclopedia / edited by Ann Kovalchick and Kara Dawson
Santa Barbara, Calif. : ABC-CLIO, c2004
Connect to
Electronic resource
2 v. in 1: ill. 27 cm
Includes bibliographical references and index
Electronic reproduction. Boulder, Colo. : NetLibrary, 2003. Available via World Wide Web. Access may be limited to NetLibrary affiliated libraries

FIGURE 4.1. OPAC view of a NetLibrary e-book bibliographic record.

Selecting and Ordering Material

Workflow procedures for creating and placing orders differ among libraries, and specific processes vary among systems. However, some practices are common throughout libraries.

Library acquisitions departments receive requests to order material in a number of ways. The requests may come as paper slips or on pre-printed forms, from e-mail, or electronic forms on the library's Web site that link into the library system. Electronic requests enable staff to import the information directly into the order record without re-keying the request data, thus speeding up the order-creation process.

Different types of orders exist. A monograph order is for a stand-alone, once-only publication that may have multiple parts such as a book, a movie, or a recording. A serial or subscription order is for a publication issued in regular or irregular parts, such as a journal or newspaper to which a library subscribes. Standing orders are continuing orders for monographs published regularly, for example, series that include separately published titles on specific subjects such as business, mathematics, and science.

To order an item, acquisitions staff may proceed as follows:

1. Search the library online catalog. If the item is already held in the library, order an additional copy or copies, or if the request is for a more recent edition, obtain relevant details for a new order.
2. If the requested item is not already in the library, create or download a bibliographic record.
3. Secure a license and determine access methods, i.e., if material is in electronic format such as electronic journals, online databases, or e-books.
4. Verify the correct bibliographic details such as title, author, publisher and date, ISBN, and price by searching a bibliographic utility's, vendor's, or publisher's online database or online library catalog.
5. Select an appropriate vendor based on availability and urgency of the request.
6. Select a fund to charge the expenditure against.

Bibliographic Records

The bibliographic record, the first record added to the system database, includes brief descriptive details for the item—title, author, publisher, date of publication, and ISBN or ISSN.

Options for adding bibliographic records are:

1. Use the Web or the Z39.50 communication protocol to search a bibliographic utility, vendor database, or other catalog for a bibliographic record. Download or export records into the local library system one at a time, or download multiple records in a batch or group. Some vendors offer one-stop options on their Web sites for verifying and placing orders, and for exporting MARC bibliographic records into the library system.
2. If a bibliographic record is not available, create a brief "on-the-fly" bibliographic record for updating later, or a full bibliographic record.

Figure 4.2 shows the options in the first step in the ordering process.

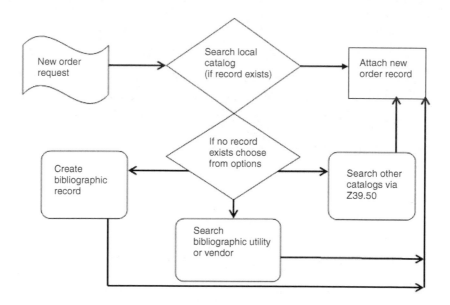

FIGURE 4.2. Options for adding bibliographic and order records.

Orders

The order data include fund, vendor, format of material, order date, price, currency, number of copies, and library location, such as branch or department. Options for creating orders in different systems include:

1. Attach a new order record to the bibliographic record.
2. The system uses order details embedded in local MARC fields in bibliographic records and creates an order as the bibliographic record is imported. The local system assigns fund encumbrances.
3. Order data are stored in the bibliographic record.

The system allocates a unique purchase order number for the order that is searchable in the database. The purchase order number is used as a reference in communication with vendors and for matching with invoices for payment.

If the order is for an additional copy of an item, staff can copy and edit the original order data, or create new order data in a record or within the bibliographic record depending on the system. In both cases the record contains updated data relevant to the current order. A new bibliographic record is needed if the order is for a more recent edition, or if a newer edition is discovered during the verification process.

Record Templates

Library systems require templates or preset work forms to create new records. Multiple templates for different situations incorporate vendor, location, type of material, type of order, and statistical information. The record creation process is fast when template data are inserted automatically into the records.

An order record stores vendor, location, date, and statistical information in fixed or brief fields. Variable-length fields contain longer bibliographic descriptive data in MARC or other formats. Free text-variable-length fields store internal processing and vendor notes, and arrival notification details. Figure 4.3 shows an order record with fixed fields displayed in the table grid. The variable-length fields

SYSTEM NO	122833456					
LOCATION Junior fic	PAYMENT	ORDER DATE 5.12.2005	NOTES Urgent	RECEIVE	COPIES 5	
FUND jfic	VENDOR ABP	DELIVERY Acq	STATUS O/o	PRICE $27.99	TYPE Book	
AUTHOR	Rowling J.K.					
TITLE	Harry Potter and the half–blood prince : Drago, Dormiens, Nunquam, Titillandus / J. K. Rowling.					
PUBLISHER	Bloomsbury Publishing Plc					
DATE	2005					
PLACE	London					
ISBN	0747581088					

FIGURE 4.3. Typical bibliographic record with order details.

Location and Fund with multiple codes are expansions of the value *multi* in the Location and Fund fixed fields.

Sending Orders

Within the acquisitions module libraries define the order details to be sent, for example, title, author, publishing data, number of copies, type of order (e.g., "rush"), and the estimated price. The system may process and send orders to vendors in a batch or one at a time. Options for sending orders to vendors are:

- print, mail, or fax purchase order (PO) forms
- send PO forms via electronic mail using the BISAC standard
- transmit files of PO forms via FTP using the EDIFACT standard

The system extracts postal and e-mail addresses from the vendor record and inserts them in the purchase order. Both electronic methods (BISAC and EDIFACT) are fast and do not incur paper, printing, and postage costs. Data are sent directly to vendors' electronic mailboxes or databases for downloading into the vendor software.

The system updates the order as it is sent to a vendor. If staff members place an order outside the library system by phone or fax, they annotate the record manually to indicate an order was placed. For orders placed directly via a shopping cart or basket on a vendor's Web site, some systems can import MARC bibliographic records with embedded order data, and conversion of the information into purchase orders.

Library staff can view an order record in the system at any time to check its status, and the public can see that an item is on order through the OPAC, as shown in Figure 4.4.

Receive Items

When ordered items arrive in acquisitions, the next step is to search for and retrieve order records from the catalog database. Personnel can record the item's arrival, and number of copies; the system adds the received date to the order record. Depending on library work procedures, the item will:

- pass to the cataloging department for updating or replacing of the original bibliographic record with a full MARC record, attaching item or holdings records, and processing the item for loan
- remain with acquisitions staff who create item records and process the item for loan, passing it to cataloging staff to update the bibliographic record
- pass to circulation staff for shelving if it came from the vendor shelf-ready

In the OPAC, a status indicator, such as *Recently Received* for new items, for a specified number of days indicates to patrons that the item is in processing. Staff can extract lists of new or recently acquired titles to display in the OPAC.

Author	Billings, Harold, 1931-
Title	**Magic & hypersystems : constructing the information-sharing library** / Harold Billings.
Published	Chicago : American Library Association, 2002.

1 copy ordered for State Ref Library on 10-04-2003.

FIGURE 4.4. OPAC view of an item on order.

CLAIM AND CANCEL ORDERS

Occasionally, vendors do not supply ordered items within the expected delivery times, for reasons such as publication or shipping delays, or communications difficulties. In such situations, libraries send claims to vendors to follow up late or not received items. Staff can choose to cancel orders that are too late, or no longer required.

Claiming

Acquisitions modules include functions that enable staff to claim late items regularly, and on an individual title or item basis. These procedures apply to the claiming of monographs or complete serial subscriptions. Claims for serials issues are managed in a separate process within the serials module (see Chapter 7).

Using the system-wide claiming process, the system can scan orders and alert staff to the order records not received, based on a number of factors:

- date the item was ordered
- normal delivery time for a vendor (as defined by the library)
- received date (blank if item is late)

For example, if an item ordered on March 1, with a normal delivery time of six weeks, is not received by May 30, the system identifies the order record for claiming. Library staff can view the record and decide whether to activate a claim, or cancel the order.

Library staff can claim items individually one at a time if an item is needed urgently or reported as late by library patrons, or if someone notices that an order is very late.

When the system prepares a claim, it generates data from the order record to send to the vendor, similar to sending purchase orders. The methods for transmitting claims to vendors are:

- printed forms sent by mail or fax
- electronic forms sent using EDI (electronic data interchange)
- claims made on a vendor's Web site
- urgent claims phoned to vendors

The system updates the record each time an order is claimed. This information is used for statistical purposes, and to advise staff of the order status of an item.

Cancellations

Sometimes library staff may decide that a late item is no longer required and choose to cancel the order. This is achieved as part of the claiming process and instead of sending a claim a cancellation notice is generated and sent.

Another cancellation procedure is when the vendor advises it is canceling an order because the item is not to be published, or cannot be obtained. Library staff may then cancel the order record and the system does not generate a notice, but instead updates the order record to note that the item was cancelled by the vendor.

FINANCIAL MANAGEMENT

Acquisitions modules may include a financial or accounting segment to track the encumbrance (commitment) and expenditure (payment) of orders against funds. Fund management, invoice payment, fiscal or financial closing functions, and reporting options make up this segment. The financial management segment does not need to replace an organization's official accounting procedures, but it may follow the same fund structure and interact with other online accounting programs.

Fund Accounts

Within the financial module staff can create multiple fund records representing the format of materials, geographic or branch locations, or other breakdowns appropriate to the local needs. As libraries receive annual budgets from their parent organizations authorized staff can add monetary amounts to the funds. Records may include internal organizational account details for tracking purposes.

At the end of a fiscal or financial year, the system's fiscal close function is implemented according to the financial or auditing requirements. Outstanding encumbrances, material ordered but not yet received, can be carried over into the next year's funds and fund balances are set to zero to be ready for appropriation of amounts in the new financial year. If libraries cannot carry over outstanding orders, another option is to create a new set of fund records and appropriations, keeping the old funds to record the payment of outstanding encumbrances.

Currency Conversion

Libraries that purchase materials in foreign currencies use a currency conversion table in the acquisitions module to convert prices to the local currency of the system. Library staff must update the conversion rates of currencies in the table on a regular basis. During the order record creation the system uses the currency table to convert the item price from its original currency to the library's local currency. The system encumbers and expends against funds in the local currency, storing both the local and foreign currency amounts in the order record and the invoice.

Paying Invoices

As items arrive in the library (and are processed by staff), the invoice function within the acquisitions module marks vendor invoices as paid. The system disencumbers or removes the estimated price amount from the encumbered fund, and charges or expends the amount paid to the fund. The system updates the order record status to indicate that it is fully paid, or partially paid if not all ordered copies arrived. Receipt and invoicing are completed together in one step, or, depending on the library's work flow, the two processes may be separate.

Some vendors offer invoicing using the Electronic Data Interchange for Administration, Commerce and Transport (EDIFACT), which enables library systems to interface with the vendor system to download invoice files into the local system. Each file contains invoices for multiple orders that are paid in a batch, doing away with the need for staff to retrieve and view each order. Both invoice and order records use unique numbers or title IDs as a match point to link the two records correctly. This is a fast, efficient method for payment of invoices. Major vendors use electronic invoicing for large serial subscription renewals, approval plans, and some monograph firm orders.

After payment of invoices on the system, the details are sent to the library or institutional accounting office for actual payment. Some systems can output a file of financial payment data to interface with the parent organization's accounting system. Libraries use invoicing and payment information for statistical reports and to answer vendor and staff inquiries.

Financial Reporting

Financial reports can be generated from the system. Fund reports include the financial balances of each fund, showing the figures for expenditure, encumbrance, and appropriation. Detailed accounting reports list every line activity for each fund, similar to a bank statement. If the system allows, fund records can be grouped into reports based on combinations of fund types such as material format, subject, or location. Authorized library staff monitor the library's budget and run financial or accounting reports on a regular basis. Staff may authorize patrons such as academic faculty to view the status of funds relevant to their departments.

REVIEW QUESTIONS

1. Name three ways a library can receive requests for items from patrons.
2. Explain why library staff would choose to create a brief bibliographic record instead of a full MARC record when ordering.
3. Name two of the standards used in electronic ordering.
4. Explain the difference between encumbrance and expenditure.

Chapter 5

Cataloging

TERMINOLOGY

AACR2: The *Anglo-American Cataloging Rules,* version 2, used by the English-speaking world to describe materials recorded in an on-line catalog.

access point: A searchable element in an online catalog record.

authority record: A record that provides the preferred version of a name, title, or subject, and related headings for a subject.

bibliographic record: A catalog record that uniquely describes a title.

bibliographic utility: An organization that distributes bibliographic records to libraries.

Dublin Core: The Dublin Core Metadata Initiative (DCMI) is a non-profit group working to define methods for the description of electronic and digital resources.

fixed-length field: A field in a catalog record containing data that are fixed in length.

FRBR (Functional Requirements for Bibliographic Records): A format that groups together bibliographic records for all manifestations of a work.

indexing: The processing of data to provide database search access points.

indicator: Numeric values added to MARC tags to provide additional cataloging information.

item record: A catalog record representing each copy of a title.

LCSH (Library of Congress Subject Headings): A controlled set of subject descriptors used to describe the subject content of titles represented in BIBLIOGRAPHIC records.

MARC (MAchine Readable Cataloging): An international standard for computerized bibliographic data developed by the Library of Congress.

metadata: Data about data; description of a digital document to improve the search and retrieval of records representing the document.

online catalog: A computerized searchable database of library material.

OPAC (Online Public Access Catalog): The public view of the ONLINE CATALOG.

overlay: The process of replacing a bibliographic record by downloading another, matching on a unique control or identifier number.

PURL (Persistent Uniform Resource Locator): An intermediate resolution service that associates a PURL with the actual URL and returns that URL to the client.

subfield: A smaller element or segment of a record field.

subject heading: The subject description of a title, assigned from an established list of headings, e.g., LCSH.

tag: The element of a MARC record that indicates a field, for example title or subject.

Unicode: An international encoding system that stores and represents multiple language characters in online systems.

uniform title: The standard title for a work that represents multiple variations, e.g., the uniform title *the Bible* represents many versions of the work.

variable-length field: A field containing data of any length.

THE ONLINE CATALOG

In an integrated library system the online catalog is the main database, containing records that represent material held within a library and electronic resources to which a library has access. The online catalog is the finding tool for patrons to locate and access resources. A catalog may be shared by multiple libraries in a library consortium, and libraries may link their catalogs together in a shared union catalog. The online catalog database is updated in real time to reflect new items ordered and added to the library's resources.

ONLINE CATALOGING STANDARDS

The primary standards used in the creation of online cataloging records are the MARC record format, the AACR2 rules, and metadata schemes.

MARC Format

The MARC (MAchine Readable Cataloging) format enables cataloging or descriptive metadata in a bibliographic record to be read by a computer (machine). The United States Library of Congress developed the MARC format in the 1960s to enable the conversion of catalog cards to computer formats. The adoption of MARC by libraries standardized the transfer of bibliographic records among integrated library systems. LCMARC, the original format, evolved into the international standard MARC 21. The Library of Congress and the National Library of Canada together form the MARC 21 maintenance agency. MARC 21 is used in Australia, Canada, New Zealand, the United Kingdom, as well as the United States. Other versions include

UNIMARC (Europe), and Chinese MARC (China, Hong Kong, and Taiwan).

MARC defines formats for bibliographic, item or holding, and authority records. It is the preferred format for the exchange of records among bibliographic utilities, vendors, and library catalogs, and for the conversion of records between library systems. However, library systems also allow for the creation of non-MARC records, and some libraries prefer to use non-MARC formats. A brief non-MARC bibliographic record is often created at the time of ordering and is replaced by a full MARC record when items arrive. Although not all staff have to create complete records in MARC, understanding the structure and function of the MARC format is essential if you are working with bibliographic records.

MARC Record Structure

The elements of a MARC record are as follows:

Field. Each piece of information is stored in a separate field within a MARC record. A field has a numerical MARC tag that corresponds to a predefined label such as title, author, or subject.

Tag. A three-digit number at the beginning of a field. Groups of tags represent fields with similar data, for example:

- tags beginning with 1 contain main entry data for a work, author, e.g., 100 for personal names, 110 for author corporate names, 130 for uniform title (e.g., the Bible)
- fields beginning with 24 tags contain titles, e.g., 245 for main title, 240 for a uniform title that is not a main entry
- fields in the 600 tag group contain subject heading data, e.g., 600 for a subject personal name entry, 650 for a topical subject entry, 651 for a geographic subject entry

Tag groups are referred to as 1XX, 2XX, 5XX, 6XX, for example:

0XX   Control information, numbers, codes to indicate information such as target audience, format, frequency, cataloging source, standard numbers (ISBN, ISSN)

1XX   Main entry, i.e., name (author), uniform title

2XX   Title, statement of responsibility, edition, imprint (publication data)

3XX Physical description
4XX Series statements (e.g., *Harvard Business Review* book series)
5XX Notes, such as Bibliography, Contents
6XX Subject headings, added entries
7XX Author or title added entries
8XX Series added entries, electronic access
9XX Local data such as holdings, barcode, order details.

Indicator. Two single-digit numbers with values from 0-9 appearing after the tag to provide further instructions to the system about how to process the following data. For example, the tag and indicator combination 24510 instructs the system to make an added title index entry in the catalog when a 1XX tag group is the main entry.

Subfield. A field is divided into subfields to define separate pieces of information. A subfield is indicated by a subfield delimiter such as | or $ and a subfield code, a lower-case alphabetical letter. For example, |c, or $c defines the author element of a title field.

For example, in the following MARC fields

24510|a Metadata fundamentals for all librarians / |cPriscilla Caplan
260 |aChicago :|bAmerican Library Association,|c2003.

Field 245 breaks into title and statement of responsibility; 260 includes place of publication, publisher, and date published.

Leader. The leader is the first twenty-four characters of a MARC record. Each position has a meaning that the computer uses to process the record such as type of tiem, bibliographic level (serial or monograph) and length of record.

Directory. A MARC record is stored in the system as a long string of data that is not in separate, tagged fields. The library system constructs a directory from cataloging data in the bibliographic record. The directory tells the system which tags are in a record and where to place them by counting characters to the position where each field, subfield, and data begins and ends. The directory is stored after the leader.

For a good explanation of the MARC format see the tutorial Understanding MARC Bibliographic: MAchine Readable Cataloging at <http://www.loc.gov/marc/umb/>.

MARC Record Display

Catalog records within system staff modules display in full MARC editing mode. Cataloging staff can toggle or switch to the OPAC to see a public display of a record. The OPAC provides a briefer, simplified version of the record with numeric MARC tags translated to customized labels such as Author, Title, and Subject. Most OPACs offer a MARC view of a record, sometimes called staff or view, but the public can view only, not edit or change catalog records. Figures 5.1 and 5.2 show a catalog record in the OPAC and its corresponding MARC record display.

AACR2

The *Anglo-American Cataloging Rules,* version 2 (AACR2) show how to describe materials in an online catalog record. The rules, published by American, Canadian, and British library associations, have instructions for each MARC field, subfields, MARC tag indicators, punctuation, and how to determine the access or search points in a catalog. For example, MARC fields 100, 245, 260, and 300 (author, title, publisher, and description) in Figure 5.2 are formatted according to the AACR2 rules.

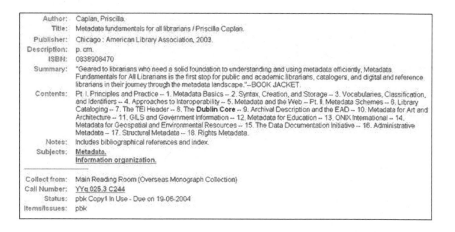

Author:	Caplan, Priscilla.
Title:	Metadata fundamentals for all librarians / Priscilla Caplan.
Publisher:	Chicago : American Library Association, 2003.
Description:	p. cm.
ISBN:	0838908470
Summary:	"Geared to librarians who need a solid foundation to understanding and using metadata efficiently, Metadata Fundamentals for All Librarians is the first stop for public and academic librarians, catalogers, and digital and reference librarians in their journey through the metadata landscape."--BOOK JACKET.
Contents:	Pt. I. Principles and Practice -- 1. Metadata Basics -- 2. Syntax, Creation, and Storage -- 3. Vocabularies, Classification, and Identifiers -- 4. Approaches to Interoperability -- 5. Metadata and the Web -- Pt. II. Metadata Schemes -- 6. Library Cataloging -- 7. The TEI Header -- 8. The **Dublin Core** -- 9. Archival Description and the EAD -- 10. Metadata for Art and Architecture -- 11. GILS and Government Information -- 12. Metadata for Education -- 13. ONIX International -- 14. Metadata for Geospatial and Environmental Resources -- 15. The Data Documentation Initiative -- 16. Administrative Metadata -- 17. Structural Metadata -- 18. Rights Metadata.
Notes:	Includes bibliographical references and index.
Subjects:	Metadata. Information organization.
Collect from:	Main Reading Room (Overseas Monograph Collection)
Call Number:	YYq 025.3 C244
Status:	pbk Copy1 In Use - Due on 19-06-2004
Items/Issues:	pbk

FIGURE 5.1. OPAC view of a library record.

```
000   01761nam 22002898a 450
001   2381890
005   20031007210230.0
008   021023s2003 ilu b 001 0 eng
010   __ |a 2002151683
019   1_ |a 24183583 |z 24183583
020   __ |a 0838906470
035   __ |9 000024183583
035   __ |9 3383362
040   __ |a DLC |b eng |c DLC |d OrLoB-B |d DLC
050   00 |a Z666.5 |b .C37 2003
082   00 |a 025.3 |2 21
100   1_ |a Caplan, Priscilla.
245   10 |a Metadata fundamentals for all librarians / |c Priscilla Caplan.
260   __ |a Chicago : |b American Library Association, |c 2003.
263   __ |a 0302
300   __ |a p. cm.
504   __ |a Includes bibliographical references and index.
505   0_ |a Pt. I. Principles and Practice -- 1. Metadata Basics -- 2. Syntax, Creation, and Storage -- 3. Vocabularies, Classification, and.
      Identifiers -- 4. Approaches to Interoperability -- 5. Metadata and the Web -- Pt. II. Metadata Schemes -- 6. Library Cataloging -- 7. The
      TEI Header -- 8. The Dublin Core -- 9. Archival Description and the EAD -- 10. Metadata for Art and Architecture -- 11. GILS and
      Government Information -- 12. Metadata for Education -- 13. ONIX International -- 14. Metadata for Geospatial and Environmental
      Resources -- 15. The Data Documentation Initiative -- 16. Administrative Metadata -- 17. Structural Metadata -- 18. Rights Metadata.
520   1_ |a "Geared to librarians who need a solid foundation to understanding and using metadata efficiently, Metadata Fundamentals for
      All Librarians is the first stop for public and academic librarians, catalogers, and digital and reference librarians in their journey through
      the metadata landscape."--BOOK JACKET.
650   _0 |a Metadata.
650   _0 |a Information organization.
984   __ |a ANL |c YYq 025.3 C244
```

FIGURE 5.2. MARC view of the record in Figure 5.1.

Metadata

When libraries began creating catalog records for Internet and other digital publications, they found that existing cataloging standards were not adequate for describing electronic resources. This led to the establishment in 1995 of the Dublin Core Metadata Initiative (DCMI) by OCLC and the National Center for Supercomputing Applications (NCSA), joined later by other countries and organizations. DCMI developed a set of standard metadata elements to use for describing digital resources.

DCMI metadata expands and builds on standard MARC fields. The original fifteen metadata elements are

1. title
2. creator
3. subject
4. description
5. contributor
6. date

7. type (genre)
8. format (file type)
9. identifier (URL, ISBN)
10. source (derived from)
11. language
12. relation (to other resources)
13. coverage (e.g., spatial)
14. source
15. management rights

The original set has been expanded. Metadata schemes are adaptable, unlike MARC. Organizations adapt the Dublin Core set to create metadata schemes for digital documents to suit different user communities. Web sites include descriptive metadata tags to improve retrieval by Web search engines. More information about using metadata is available from the Dublin Core Web site <http://dublincore.org>.

Other metadata schema include:

*   the Global Information Locator Service (GILS), which is used in government organizations,
*   the Metadata Encoding and Transmission Standard (METS) for describing digital objects, and
*   the Metadata Object Description Schema (MODS), which extends and changes elements from MARC 21.

Both METS and MODS are developed by the Library of Congress. Many organisations adapt and enhance standard metadata schema to incorporate local information.

Cataloging Tools

The *Catalogers' Desktop* is a comprehensive electronic collection of cataloging tools for use by cataloging staff. It includes the *AACR2 Cataloging Rules,* Library of Congress Rule Interpretations, MARC21 Formats, lists of MARC codes, and links to metadata resources. The *Catalogers' Desktop* is available in CD-ROM format, and on the Web. See the Library of Congress Catalogers' Desktop Web site <http://www.loc.gov/cds/desktop/>.

BIBLIOGRAPHIC UTILITIES

A bibliographic utility is an agency or organization that distributes cataloging records and other services to subscribing libraries. The utility databases include bibliographic records from the Library of Congress and other national libraries, as well as original bibliographic records contributed by member libraries.

OCLC, the Online Computer Library Center, is a large, nonprofit organization serving thousands of libraries in the United States and other countries. WorldCat is the primary OCLC bibliographic database of catalog records. In addition, it provides authority records, retrospective conversion, contract cataloging, Arabic, Chinese, Japanese, and Korean (CJK) cataloging. Member libraries use OCLC cataloging software tools such as Connexion, CatME, and CatExpress to create, edit, search, and download bibliographic and authority records. PromptCat supplies copy cataloging records and shelf-ready material in conjunction with vendors. Find out more about OCLC at its Web site <http://www.oclc.org>.

RLG, the Research Libraries Group, is a nonprofit cooperative organization of academic, national, archival, and research libraries, and museums. RLG provides RLIN, the Research Libraries Information Network, a specialized international bibliographic database service that accesses the RLG Union Catalog and other services. RLG also provides authority records, archival resources, records in Arabic, Chinese, Cyrillic, Hebrew, Japanese, and Korean scripts, gateways to union catalogs from Germany, Australia, CURL (Consortium of UK Research Libraries in the United Kingdom), the English Short Title Catalogue (ESTC), and SCIPIO: the Art and Rare Books Catalog, and subject-based reference databases. Find out more about RLG at <http://www.rlg.org>.

National libraries in other countries provide bibliographic utility services, for example, the National Library of Australia's Libraries Australia (previously Kinetica), and the British Library's National Bibliographic Service.

CATALOG RECORDS

Three record types are associated with cataloging: the bibliographic record, the authority record, and the item or holdings record.

Bibliographic and item records form the core of the catalog and are accessible from other modules. Staff members access different record types based on their workflow and user authorizations. For example, acquisitions staff may be authorized to create brief bibliographic records, or download bibliographic records from another system, but not to delete full bibliographic records. Cataloging staff have different levels of authorization for the functions associated with maintaining bibliographic records.

Bibliographic Records

A bibliographic record is a description of the work it represents. It contains sufficient detail to identify the title uniquely from other titles. For example, if a title is published once, and then revised and republished as another edition at a later date, a separate bibliographic record is created for the revised edition. The structure and description of a bibliographic record follow the MARC format and the *Anglo-American Cataloging Rules, Second Edition, Revised* (AACR2). The FRBR (Functional Requirements for Bibliographic Records) model groups together bibliographic records for manifestations of one work so that a single search retrieves all related materials even if cataloged in different languages or using different subject headings.

A bibliographic record includes fields of fixed and variable length. Fixed-length fields store coded data such as language, country of publication, medium, or format. Each field has a specified or fixed length, such as a three-letter code for language, or a two-letter code for country. Fixed-length fields do not display in the public catalog, but their data are used to limit searches in the online catalog, and to provide statistical reports for library staff. For example, by using coded data stored in fixed fields:

- patrons can limit a search to books in the Russian language; or
- staff can create a report on the number of videos or DVDs in Spanish language held in a library.

Variable-length fields contain descriptive data for a work and are greater in length than fixed fields, up to a number of characters set by the library system (letters, numbers, and spaces are all counted as characters). Examples of variable-length fields (MARC or non-MARC) include the following:

- Title, statement of responsibility (e.g., author, editor, director), edition, publication information, physical description, series, notes, table of contents, and international standard numbers, following the AACR2 rules.
- Main and added access points that enable retrieval of a record from the online catalog. AACR2 rules determine the main entry, and added entries. A main entry is the first field that displays in a bibliographic record. For example, an edited, multiauthored work has a title main entry because no single author has full responsibility. However, both main and added entries are access points in the online catalog, so that a record is retrieved if you search by title, author, editor, director, illustrator, composer, or subject.
- Subject headings describing the content of the title, selected from an established thesaurus or established set of controlled subject headings such as *Library of Congress Subject Headings (LCSH), Sears List of Subject Headings (Sears),* or *Medical Subject Headings (MeSH).*
- A call number assigned using a classification scheme such as the Dewey Decimal System or Library of Congress, grouping similar items by subject on a physical shelf, or in a call-number search of the online catalog.
- Notes about the work providing additional information such as Contents, Bibliography, Summary.

Variable-length fields are repeatable. For example, a record may have multiple subject headings, more than one added entry for title, author, editor, director, illustrator, composer, and additional descriptive or explanatory notes.

Item or Holding Records

The item or holding record represents each physical copy of a title held in a library, including branches. The record's data indicate where a copy is located, the media type or format, and the date the copy was added to the library system. When a copy circulates, the item record interacts with the library system's circulation module, storing details of the borrowing patron, date checked out and in, as well as other statistical data. An item record has multiple fixed fields that store

Harry Potter and the chamber of secrets / J. K. Rowling.		Item Type:	Junior Fiction
Author: Rowling, J. K.		Status:	Available
Call No: JF ROWL		Home:	Avalon
		Currently:	Avalon
Harry Potter and the chamber of secrets / J. K. Rowling.		Item Type:	Junior Fiction
Author: Rowling, J. K.		Status:	On Loan
Call No: JF ROWL		Home:	Avalon
		Currently:	Avalon
Harry Potter and the chamber of secrets / J. K. Rowling.		Item Type:	Junior Fiction
Author: Rowling, J. K.		Status:	Available
Call No: JF ROWL		Home:	Avalon
		Currently:	Avalon

FIGURE 5.3. OPAC search result displaying brief bibliographic information listed by title, and item information at the right.

library-coded and system-generated data. Variable-length fields contain barcode data, internal processing and historical notes about the item, and volume information for serials and multivolume sets. Chapter 6 has further information on item records.

Acquisitions or cataloging staff create item records as copies are received in the library, according to individual library workflows. A single bibliographic record can have multiple items attached, representing all the copies held throughout a library. Figure 5.3 shows bibliographic data combined with information from item records in an OPAC, indicating that the library holds multiple copies of the title.

Barcodes

A unique barcode creates a link between the item and record. The physical barcode attaches to the item in an easily accessible place, and when scanned the system reads the number from the physical barcode into the item record. At checkout, circulation staff use a barcode scanner (handheld or fixed to the computer) to read the number into the library system and retrieve the item record. Barcodes placed on the outside of a physical copy reduce physical wear on both the item and circulation staff (no need to open the cover), and facilitate self-checkout and self-checkin of material by library patrons.

Authority Records

Authority records provide consistency in names and subjects in a library database in the following ways:

1. If a particular name or subject is used in the catalog, an authority record links variations of that name or subject to the authorized or preferred heading. This is called a *See* reference. For example, in Figure 5.4 the entry Financial Crashes—See Financial Crises means the heading Financial Crises is used instead of Financial Crashes in the catalog.
2. A *See also* authority record links related topics or names. For example, in Figure 5.4 Financial Crises—2 Related Subjects is a *See also* link that displays related subject headings when selected.
3. When catalogers create new bibliographic records they consult an authority file or authority records for the authorized name or subject heading. This ensures that multiple variations of the same heading are not added to the database.
4. Catalogers create new authority records to reflect local and current topical authority needs, such as names or events.

Authority records have a structure similar to MARC bibliographic records. The following numeric MARC tags instruct the online system how to display the records in the catalog:

1XX	Headings
2XX	Complex See Reference
3XX	Complex See Also Reference—Subject
4XX	See From Tracing Fields
5XX	See Also From Tracing Fields
6XX	Complex See and See Also References; Series Treatment; Notes
7XX	Heading Linking Entries
8XX	Other Variable Fields

Financial Accounting -- See --**Accounting**
--subdivision Accounting under topics, e.g. Dairying--Accounting; Corporations--Accounting; and under names of individual corporate bodies
Financial Aid Student -- See --**Student Aid**
Financial Aid To Students -- See --**Student Aid**
Financial Crashes -- See --**Financial Crises**
Financial Crimes -- See --**Commercial Crimes**
Financial Crises -- 2 Related Subjects

FIGURE 5.4. Examples of authority references in a public online catalog.

Libraries can create authority records within the cataloging module, and purchase batches of records from a source such as OCLC or the Library of Congress for downloading to a local library system.

CATALOGING WORKFLOW

Two methods can be used for adding bibliographic records to the online catalog. Copy cataloging describes the process of downloading bibliographic records from utilities or vendor online systems. This is the most popular method in many libraries. Creating complete, new bibliographic records from scratch is known as original cataloging.

Copy Cataloging

Many libraries download bibliographic records directly to local online catalogs from a bibliographic utility such as OCLC or RLIN, a commercial vendor database, or another library's online catalog. Copy cataloging is often the responsibility of library technicians in cataloging departments when items arrive, or in acquisitions departments at the time of ordering.

Downloading Records

Utility or vendor databases can be accessed via a Web site, or a Z39.50 communications link from the local system. The procedures for obtaining bibliographic records are:

1. Search the utility database using standard numbers (ISBN or ISSN), title, or author, and select a bibliographic record whose description matches the item being ordered or cataloged.
2. Locate the correct bibliographic record for export or downloading to the local catalog using procedures of both the local and external systems. If item data such as barcodes, shelf locations, and prices are added to a MARC field in the bibliographic record the local system converts that data into item records as it downloads the record.

3. Download records individually, one at a time, or transfer a batch or group from the bibliographic utility or vendor to the local system using the Internet file transfer protocol (FTP).

Load Profiles

When bibliographic records download into the local library catalog they pass through a predefined profile that converts the records into the format for the local system. Libraries define the profile, specifying the fields and subfields they wish to keep in the record. The system removes fields not needed while adding them to the catalog. For example, a library may want to change the MARC tag of incoming call numbers to a different MARC tag, or if there are two call number fields in the record, keep only one. Multiple profiles for different utilities or vendors can be established.

The downloaded bibliographic record is often more up-to-date than the record created at the time the title was ordered. In this instance the load profile has instructions to overlay an existing record with the new bibliographic record. Overlaying uses a unique control number in the record as a match point, for example, an OCLC or utility number, or an existing record number. The overlay procedure prevents the addition of multiple records for the same title to the database.

After downloading, cataloging staff edit bibliographic records, adding information such as local call numbers, or additional subject headings. For each copy of a title staff add an item record or the system uses embedded item data to create a record as part of the download.

Original Cataloging

If a title is recently published or has a specialized topic, for example, local or government publications, a bibliographic record may not exist in a utility or vendor database. In these cases the library uses original cataloging to create a full bibliographic record directly on the local system. Catalogers analyze the publication and create a new bibliographic record using the MARC and AACR2 formats to describe the title. They select subject headings from established subject heading lists such as the *Library of Congress Subject Headings*

(LCSH), Sears List of Subject Headings, or *Medical Subject Headings (MeSH).* A record contains as many subject headings as are needed for its description. Each heading becomes a search or access point in the online catalog.

Cataloging staff or a separate processing team attaches item records to the bibliographic record for each copy of a title received in the library. Checking in items to the circulation system activates their borrowing status. Figure 5.5 shows the online cataloging workflow options.

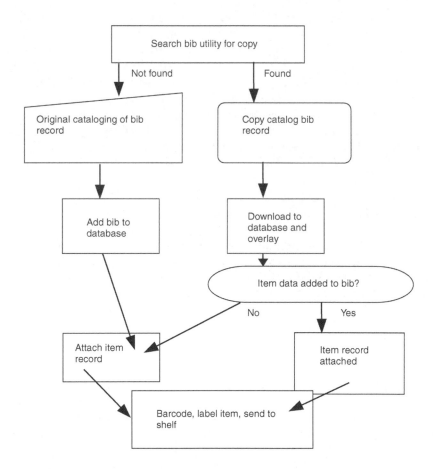

FIGURE 5.5. Online cataloging workflow options.

Generating Labels

In the processing of item records the cataloging module can be used to print labels. Two kinds of labels are:

1. spine labels that display a call number visible from a shelf (narrow); and
2. pocket labels with title and barcode or call number to place inside an item (wide).

The term *pocket label* refers to labels on a circulation card pocket. Libraries no longer use card pockets, but some still add a pocket-sized label to items.

System options allow libraries to specify label size and the data to print for different types of materials. The system uses these settings when generating labels for printing either individually or in a batch, based on record type or other parameters.

The addition of new records to the library system, by both copy and original cataloging methods, makes use of preestablished record templates. A record template defines the fields needed in each record type, and can include data such as punctuation, subfield codes, location codes, notes, or series statements. The system stores multiple templates, defined for different types of materials (books, videos, journals) and library locations (branches, campuses). When downloading records, the system selects a default template from the loading profile, or staff can specify another template.

As the system saves each record it allocates a unique record number to be used at any time to retrieve the record from the database. The system refers to this number when reporting that a record is locked, already in use, or has been deleted from the database.

Indexing of Records

When a library installs a system, a key task is to determine the MARC fields and subfields to index for searching purposes, and the data to add to each index. This is known as an indexing profile. For example, titles, additional titles, and series titles may be in the title index as well as the keyword index. Library systems have standard indexing profiles that libraries review and change to meet local needs.

The system adds data from each record to the preestablished indexes, following the index profile. The indexes provide search access points such as author, title, subject, call number, and keyword for the staff and public in the catalog. Indexed data are immediately searchable in the catalog. See Chapter 8 for more explanation of indexing and searching.

Cataloging Digital Resources

Traditionally, a library collection and the catalog include books, journals, audiovisual, and other material held within a library that circulates in and out of the library. A growing portion of library collections includes digitized material or e-journals, Web sites, and e-books linked from the Internet. This material makes up a library's virtual collection; it is not in hard copy form and does not circulate. Patrons access the material through hypertext links in the online catalog, and because digital items do not circulate they require an item record.

Strategies for cataloging digital resources include the following.

- The incorporation of Internet addresses or URLs into bibliographic MARC field 856 which appears as a hypertext link in the public record. Figure 5.6 shows an OPAC and a MARC view of an 856 field.
- Regular maintenance of URLs using checking tools and PURLs (Persistent Uniform Resource Locators), an intermediary service that maintains changing URLs by redirecting users to a current URL.
- The linking of media files in local 9XX fields in bibliographic records.
- The inclusion of metadata descriptive fields into bibliographic records, using Dublin Core and other metadata schemes.
- Consultation with systems staff for technical advice on access.
- Licensing, authorization, and restriction considerations.

Multilingual Cataloging

Libraries may collect material in multiple languages, catalog and display bibliographic records in their original language or script or

---

Title: Scholarly electronic publishing resources [electronic resource].
Linked Resources: http://info.lib.uh.edu/sepb/sepr.htm
Publisher: Houston, Tx. : University of Houston Libraries, 1996-

---

245 00 |a Scholarly electronic publishing resources |h [electronic resource].
856 40 |u http://info.lib.uh.edu/sepb/sepr.htm
260 __ |a Houston, Tx. : |b University of Houston Libraries, 1996-

---

FIGURE 5.6. OPAC and MARC view of an 856 field containing a hypertext URL.

transliterated into roman script. Library systems manage the use of multilingual records and scripts in the following ways:

- input of cataloging data directly in an item's original script or language;
- index the data in scripts or languages to enable searching in the language or script; and
- display of records in the OPAC and staff database in original scripts or languages.

The representation of diacritic or special character sets in computers is managed by a system called Unicode, an international standardized encoding system that enables the storage of multiple character sets. Unicode provides a unique number or diacritic code for every character, and every software platform, program, or language. Most Web browsers incorporate Unicode and display multiple character sets, for example, Arabic, Chinese, Cyrillic, Japanese, Korean, or Hebrew.

Microsoft Windows and other computer operating systems include options to change keyboard language settings to enable the input of multiple character scripts. Some library systems accept this method of data input as well. Programs such as Big5 and GB traditional for Chinese, Korean Windows, or a Thai terminal emulator enable the direct input of characters in their original script. In both situations the library system software receives an encoded character according to the input method and stores it as a unique diacritic code.

Database Maintenance

Ongoing maintenance of catalog records to correct errors, and delete bibliographic, item, and authority records is an essential part of keeping the catalog current. Staff can edit records one at a time or in a group using system tools for editing multiple records simultaneously. For example, if a subject heading requires change, a global change updates all records that contain the heading. Maintenance takes place on a regular basis, by catalogers and library technicians.

REVIEW QUESTIONS

1. What is the function of the MARC format?
2. What is metadata used for?
3. Name the three types of records used in the cataloging module.
4. Give two examples of a digital resource.

Chapter 6

Circulation

TERMINOLOGY

barcode: A unique number stored in records and as a label on items and patron cards; used to retrieve records from a database.

bibliographic record: A record that uniquely describes a title.

claims returned: The status of an item that a patron claimed was returned, but the return is not recorded in the circulation system.

fixed field: A record field containing data of a fixed or specified length.

holding record: A system record representing item copies; also called an ITEM RECORD.

inventory: A stock take of library material on shelves.

item record: A representation of each circulating copy of a title; also called a HOLDING RECORD.

loan rules: Library-defined rules that prescribe different loan periods and conditions.

patron block table: A library-defined table that specifies conditions for limiting patron borrowing.

patron record: A representation of a borrower or user of a library system.

RFID (radio frequency identification): A method of tracking items for circulation, INVENTORY, and security that uses microchips.

variable-length field: A field containing data that is variable or unpredictable in length; usually has an upper character limit.

Circulation is the most complex and busiest module in the integrated library system and incorporates multiple variations in library loan policies and procedures. The role of the circulation system is to record, track, and manage the usage of library material, including checking out and in of material, reservations or holds, and the tracking of overdue items.

CIRCULATION OVERVIEW

The circulation process involves the interaction of data from multiple files and tables in the system. Patron records contain coded values indicating types of patrons, defined by the library, for example, adult and juvenile borrowers, or faculty and students. The system uses the values to apply different lending privileges. Item or holding records indicate the type of material and specific location for different borrowing options. Library staff determine parameters for rules such as loan periods for combinations of patrons, items, and locations, and other lending conditions.

During a checkout transaction, barcodes are scanned to retrieve patron and item records. The system consults a patron block table to check if a patron should be limited or blocked from borrowing. Extracting the required patron and item data from the records, the system consults the loan rule table, and finds a matching loan rule under which it checks out the item. Figure 6.1 shows a typical circulation checkout procedure.

CIRCULATION RECORDS

The primary records used in circulation transactions are patron, and item or holdings records. The system links these records together during circulation of items.

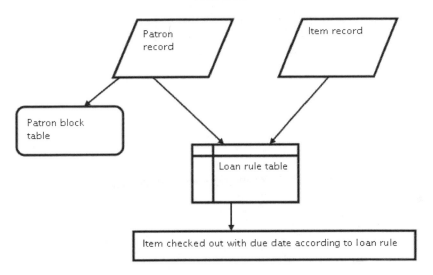

FIGURE 6.1. Circulation checkout transaction process.

Patron Records

People who wish to borrow material from a library, or access electronic resources such as e-books, e-journals, and research databases must first register as a patron or borrower. Patrons include individuals within a library's membership or clientele, other libraries, and organizations that borrow material. One record for each patron is stored in the circulation patron database.

Three methods are used for adding patron records to the database, depending on the library and the capabilities of the library system:

1. Patrons supply data in person or on a paper application form from which library staff create records on the system.
2. Patrons register online via a Web-based form.
3. Files of patron data are loaded into the circulation module from external databases of student records in academic libraries, or staff records from employment databases.

Data stored in a patron record include identifying details such as name, postal address, telephone number, e-mail address, driver's license or other unique ID number. Libraries can add statistical data such as age, gender, language, national origin, study programs or levels of study, parent or guardian names for children, and local and historical data.

Similar to other system records, a patron record contains fixed-length fields for data such as codes and dates, and variable-length fields for name, addresses, numbers, and notes. A barcode in a variable-length field links the patron record to the same barcode on a physical library or ID card. Figure 6.2 shows an example of a patron record.

The system allocates a unique number to each patron record as it is saved on the system. Staff use the number to search for and retrieve a record, and the system uses the number when referring to a locked or busy record.

Item or Holding Records

An item or holding record must exist for each piece or copy of a title that circulates. The item record links to a bibliographic record that includes the descriptive fields such as title, author, publication, and

EXPIRES	12–12–2010	CHECKOUTS	5	
TYPE	Student	RENEWALS	2	Fixed length fields
CODE1	Arts	BIRTH DATE	1	
CODE2	Female	$$$	$0.00	

NAME
Patron, Joanne

Variable length fields

ADDRESS
12 Bank St, Mews
CA 96777

TELEPHONE
622–555–6777

BARCODE
0000222111000

EMAIL ADDRESS
jpatron@library.edu

FIGURE 6.2. Patron record showing fixed and variable fields.

subject headings. A single bibliographic record may have up to several hundred item records linked to it. For example, issues of a journal or magazine that circulate need item records; or sometimes one item record is reused for different issue loans.

An item record has multiple fixed-length fields that store permanent data such as:

- the item's usual shelving location;
- a code representing the format of the item, e.g., book, journal, video, DVD;
- price for assessing replacement costs; and
- library-defined statistical codes.

Fixed-length fields also contain system-generated circulation data that the system updates as items check in and out, are renewed, or become overdue. These data include:

- date checked out
- date item is due
- record number of patron who has checked the item out
- previous patron record numbers and date checked in
- circulation status of the item, such as On Loan, Lost, Damaged, in Transit, on Hold, Billed, Missing
- number of renewals within a loan period, and total renewals
- number of overdue notices sent
- date of last overdue notice sent
- total number of checkouts
- checkouts during statistical time periods, such as annual

The system collects fixed-field statistical data for reporting purposes. Figure 6.3 shows a typical item record. Some fields are editable by staff; the system generates and updates all other fields.

Item record variable-length fields include:

- barcodes that correspond to the item barcode label
- volume details for serials
- local call numbers
- historical or circulating notes added by staff
- system-generated notes recording data from transactions such as material lost, or claimed returned

RECORD NUMBER	112342414	DUE DATE	- - -
CATEGORY	20	OUT DATE	- - -
FORMAT	Video	CHECKOUTS	22
LOCATION	Stacks	RENEWALS	0
STATUS	Fixed length fields	PRICE	$29.00
BARCODE 30000111910123			
CALL NUMBER 671.5	Variable length fields		
NOTE Contains 1 CD. Check for CD **on** **return**			

FIGURE 6.3. Typical item or holdings record showing fixed- and variable-length fields.

Barcodes

Barcodes enable the quick retrieval of item and patron records from the database. To retrieve records, staff can scan the barcode using a barcode reader, scanner, light pen or wand, attached to a system-linked computer. Barcodes can also be keyed into the system. Barcodes use the same black-and-white-striped format used in retail outlets.

A standard barcode format is the Codabar or Code 39 design, which has 14 digits. It includes item or patron data, institution or library data, and the check digit, which is the final digit calculated from the previous digits in the barcode. An explanation of the Codabar barcode pattern is shown in Figure 6.4.

An alternative to barcodes is the radio frequency identification system (RFID). An RFID tag contains a microchip and antenna, and is programmed electronically. The RFID tag functions in a similar way to a barcode, but is read by radio frequency technology, not scanned like a barcode. Using RFID, staff can check in or out a stack of eight

Patron or item Indicator	Library unique identifier	Item or patron number	Check digit (last digit)

FIGURE 6.4. Breakdown of a barcode number.

to ten items with just a single movement. Other RFID applications are available for inventory, self-checkout, and security. RFID systems are more expensive than barcodes to implement because the tags are more costly and additional hardware, readers, sensors, and servers increase the cost. However, costs will decrease as the technology becomes more widely used.

CIRCULATION PARAMETERS AND POLICIES

Circulation systems function according to library-defined variable values. During checkout the circulation module quickly determines how long an item can be borrowed for different patrons and allocates a due date to the item record. The process happens so smoothly that it is taken for granted. How does the system make such fast decisions with no human input? How does it know that one patron can borrow an item for four weeks but another patron can borrow the same item for only two weeks? To achieve this, the system consults parameters that the library adds at the time of system implementation. The parameters include policies for loan periods, fine structure, borrowing privileges, the ability to renew, overdue penalties and notice timing, and library opening and closing dates and times. Every time a circulation transaction takes place the system invokes these parameters.

Loan Rules

Libraries policies vary for situations such as:

- how long items are checked out
- when overdue notices are sent
- amounts to fine and when for overdue material
- holds or reservations
- texts of notices
- maximum number of renewals

The system stores the policies as loan rules within the circulation module. Multiple loan rules for different situations use parameters such as patron, type of item, and the location of items. For example, in an academic library, students may have shorter loan periods than faculty. Items in course reserves have shorter loan periods than material in the main collection. Reference material, rare books, and other material that does not circulate requires a noncirculating loan rule. Each loan rule specifies the loan time and other parameters. Table 6.1 shows a selection of typical elements for loan rules for faculty and students (material in the main collection) and reserve (short-loan material in the reserve collection).

TABLE 6.1. Loan rules for faculty, students, and course reserve material.

Loan rule name	Length of loan (coded for days or hours)	Holds	Number of renewals	Number of overdue notices	Time between overdue notices	Fine amounts
Faculty (main collection)	70	Yes	2	2	14	1.00
Student (main collection)	14	Yes	1	3	7	1.00
Reserve collection (1 day)	1	No	0	3	1	4.00

When the system checks out an item it uses a specific loan rule and links that loan rule with the item record. The system reads the loan rule several times during the circulation period and takes action according to values set in the loan rule. The system consults the loan rule:

- at checkout (linking the item and the loan rule)
- when an item is selected for renewal
- when a hold is placed on the item
- when the system recalls an item
- when an item is due
- when staff prepare overdue notices
- at checkin if an item is late to assess fines

Overdue Fines and Penalties

The circulation system allows libraries to determine when patrons should pay for overdue material, how much they should pay, and for how long charges should accumulate. The parameters are flexible and can be set to charge only some patrons, or not charge at all if that is the library's choice. Fines start accumulating at a library-specified number of days after material becomes overdue, and the system adds the fines to patron records when the material is returned. If a library wants to penalize late returns, but does not want to fine or collect money, alternatives such as a system of overdue penalty points may be established.

The system generates and stores a file of overdue items. Library staff accesses this list regularly to generate overdue notices to send to patrons. The first notices are courtesy or reminders that items are overdue; a final notice has details of replacement costs due if patrons do not return items. Libraries determine the number of notices, the intervals between sending them, and the texts of the notices. Options to send notices include printing and mailing, SMS text messages, or e-mail, a popular method that reduces postage costs and enhances delivery time. Many systems allow patrons to view their circulation records through the OPAC, check due dates, renew materials, and specify their preferred method for notice delivery.

Calendars

Libraries maintain calendar tables to record variations in opening and closing dates and times for all branches or member libraries using the system. During the checkout process the circulation system consults the calendar table when calculating a due date to ensure that items will not be due on days the library is closed. Similarly, if a library lends reserve material on an hourly basis a calendar stores closing and opening hours.

CIRCULATING MATERIAL

Libraries are established so that material can be taken away from the library, as well as consulted within the library. Lending libraries such as public, corporate, and educational libraries allow registered patrons to borrow material. National and state research and reference libraries do not allow material to be removed, but consulted only within the library. In practice, all libraries offer a combination of lending and reference-only material.

Checkout

Checking out of material takes place at a client computer connected to the library server through the interface of the circulation module. The system creates a link between the patron and item records so that at any time the staff can view a patron's loans, and item records show the borrowing patron's record number. The system cancels this link when an item is checked in. Some systems store loan history so that a patron can see what he or she has borrowed, and an item's previous borrowers can be identified by library staff. These are optional features a library can choose not to activate.

When an item checks out, its status changes to indicate it is on loan, and the system assigns a due date based on the loan rule. At checkout the circulation system prints a receipt for patrons, showing the title and due date. The due date or a text message indicating the item is on loan displays in the OPAC.

Self-Checkout and Checkin

The circulation desk is the busiest area in a library. Self-checkout and checkin circulation machines can supplement staffed workstations to provide flexibility in library staffing hours. The self-checkout/ checkin machine is a circulation terminal linked to the system server; patrons scan their cards and item barcodes, and the machine consults the circulation parameters to determine a loan period. If there is a problem with either the patron or item record, the patron talks to a circulation specialist. RFID tags are well suited to self-checkout and checkin because the radio frequency technology easily reads the tags and their physical location on items is not as crucial as with barcodes.

Electronic Material

How does the circulation system interact with electronic material? Because electronic materials are virtual and not physically located within a library building, they do not circulate. E-books, e-journals, e-readings in reserve, and electronic databases under license to the library have bibliographic records in the online catalog, but no item records. Instead, to access electronic resources, patrons connect to e-resources via URLs or Internet addresses of electronic items stored in MARC field 856 that display as hypertext links in the OPAC.

Libraries use authentication methods to verify patrons who are using electronic services remotely, or outside the library building (Chapter 8 discusses authentication methods). Vendors and local system methods record and track the statistics for the use of noncirculating electronic material.

Checkin

Patrons return library material to the circulation desk, or in a "book drop" or "returns chute" located both inside and outside library buildings. Circulation modules offer several options for checking in or discharging material:

- from within a patron record, if a checkin receipt is needed, or the patron wants to pay a fine (by staff)

- from a checkin (no patron record) mode, for fast checkin of material from the book drop or chute; each barcode is scanned, or with RFID, stacks of items are checked in (by staff)
- at self-checkin machines (by patrons)

At checkin, the system immediately changes the item's status to indicate its return. If an item belongs to a different branch of the library than the one it is returned to (if the library allows this practice) the status indicates the item is in transit until it returns to the owning branch or library. Once there, the item is checked in again, changing the status to show its availability. Some systems display a message indicating items are just returned, allowing time for items to be reshelved.

Renewals

When patrons wish to extend loans this is achieved through the renewal function. Loan rules determine the renewal parameters, for example:

- the ability to renew for specified patrons or items
- length of time remaining in a loan period before renewal is possible
- number of times items may be renewed
- renewal from the date renewed, or from the original due date
- options to recall items that are renewed

Circulation staff can renew items from within the circulation module for patrons in person and over the telephone. Using an Internet connection, patrons are able to renew material through their patron records on the OPAC Web site.

Claims Returned

When a patron claims an item was returned, but the circulation module has not recorded the return, the item shows as still checked out to the patron. If the patron contacts the library, staff uses the Claims Returned function in the circulation system to record the event.

Patrons may provide an explanation when claiming returned items, such as "I know I returned it on a particular day because . . ." or "I cannot find the item anywhere so I must have returned it." Claims returned may happen because items are not checked into the system on return, or the patron has not returned an item.

In considering these circumstances, a couple of actions can be taken. If the library is in error, the Claims Returned function can check the item in, remove it from the patron record, and place its details on a missing items list. If the patron is at fault, the item remains checked out to the patron who continues to receive overdue and fines notices, and the system adds the item details to the missing items list.

Missing and Lost Items

When items are marked as missing through the Claims Returned functions or by staff after checking shelves, the system changes the item record status to display *Missing* in the catalog. On a regular basis, circulation staff generate a list of missing items from the system to take to the shelves for searching.

Occasionally, a patron reports that items are lost due to theft, floods, or fire. Items are recorded as lost and the circulation system assesses the replacement cost to bill the patron, as it changes the item status to *Lost*.

Acquisitions staff review lost and missing items, and decide whether to reorder; if so, the cycle of a library item begins again. Electronic or digital data do not get lost or go missing physically, although they can disappear from the Web or other virtual location.

Financial Activities

Fines accumulate on patron records for overdue or lost items according to library policies. Library staff can place financial charges on patron records for damaged material, photocopying charges, or database usage. If libraries allow the payment of fines or fees in the library, the option to collect money is available at checkin. Staff members receive payments and update patron records immediately. The system generates receipts and details of fines paid. If libraries do not accept payments directly and fines are paid to a bursar or financial office, library systems can interact with the financial system to import payment data. The system stores circulation financial data for review, reporting, and output to off-site agencies or storage. Some systems interact with collection agencies for the monitoring of long-overdue material.

HOLDS, REQUESTS, OR RESERVATIONS

If a patron wishes to borrow an item already on loan, the system offers options to place a hold or reservation. Holds are one of the most complex parts of a circulation system, especially for busy public libraries, and they can accommodate many variations.

Two primary types of holds are:

1. *Item-level:* the hold is placed on a specific copy of a title at a specific location
2. *Title or bibliographic-level:* the hold is placed on the copy returned soonest

Library staff can place holds on behalf of patrons, and for items needed for Reserve collections. Patrons can place holds through the OPAC. As a hold is placed, the system creates a link between the item and patron record. When the item is checked in, the system triggers the hold alerting staff that a hold exists. The item is set aside or held for a specified number of days, and the patron is notified by system-generated notices mailed or e-mailed, or by phone or automatic telephone notification.

Holds Management

Libraries can set parameters within the system for many hold situations such as:

- no holds on items if a copy is available for loan anywhere in the library
- no holds if a copy is available in the patron's home branch or library
- holds placed only on the copy in the patron's branch

Popular titles often develop a queue of patron holds. When the first hold is triggered, the system activates the hold for the next patron in the queue. Multiple holds on one title may alert library staff to consider purchasing another copy when the number of holds exceeds a library-specified threshold. Holds can be canceled or modified from within the system, and patrons can cancel holds through the OPAC.

COURSE RESERVES

Academic libraries sometimes separate high-use course material from the main collection, reserving it for shorter loan periods to share among more students. The Course Reserves subset of the circulation module offers loans for items in a reserve or short-loan collection on an hourly, overnight, or daily basis rather than weekly as for other material. Short loans are processed as follows.

- Reserves staff create a course record for each study program, including the course title or number and names of faculty associated with the course.
- Faculty members advise library staff of the items to be placed in Reserve.
- Reserves staff relocate items physically from the main collection to Reserve.
- The item catalog records link to the course record so that item records display a Reserve location.
- For photocopied articles, book chapters, and private faculty material reserve staff create bibliographic and item records with Reserve locations.
- Course Reserves is a separate search category in the online catalog where students search by course name, code, or faculty to find library material for a specific course. For example, Figure 6.5 shows two items linked to the course record Asian Art and Culture in a Course Reserves module, resulting from a search by course name.

E-reserves

The Reserves module includes options for e-reserves, also called e-readings or electronic media reserves. Libraries use this function to

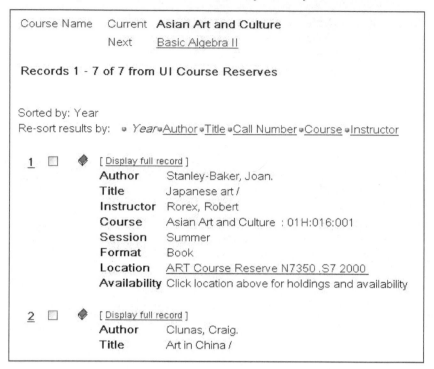

FIGURE 6.5. Items on reserve for the course Asian Art and Culture.

provide electronic or digital copies of articles and book chapters. Copies of material in PDF (Portable Document Format) and image files are stored on the system or a remote server and link to bibliographic records within the catalog. Students access e-readings from the Course Reserves module. Figure 6.6 shows a catalog entry for an e-reading.

The advantages of e-reserves are that students can view, download, or print electronic copies, according to copyright guidelines, from within or outside the library. For copyright reasons students must provide details for verification against the patron or other authentication database. Another option is password requirements at the course level so that only students enrolled in the course can view the material.

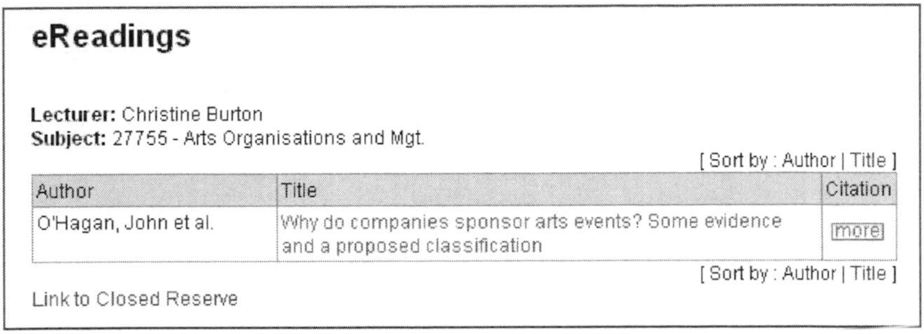

eReadings

Lecturer: Christine Burton
Subject: 27755 - Arts Organisations and Mgt.

[Sort by : Author | Title]

Author	Title	Citation
O'Hagan, John et al.	Why do companies sponsor arts events? Some evidence and a proposed classification	[more]

[Sort by : Author | Title]

Link to Closed Reserve

FIGURE 6.6. Citation details for an electronic reserve or eReading.

INVENTORY

A circulation system or module may include an option for collection stocktaking or inventory. In this subsystem, staff members use a portable barcode reader to scan items on the shelves. The barcode data are stored in a file that uploads to the system and is compared against records in the database in call number order. Staff can then identify as missing items that are not on loan, but not recorded on the shelf in the inventory list.

RFID technology is an efficient alternative for inventory procedures because the RFID tags can be read without having to remove items from the shelves.

EQUIPMENT AND MEDIA BOOKING

A media or booking facility is an optional subsystem of the circulation system. Bookings differ from holds in that patrons book an item for use at a specific time, for example, Monday 9 a.m. to 12 noon, whereas a hold is triggered only when an item is returned and checked in. Bookings are once-only or periodic, for example, at the same time and day every week in a semester.

The library determines items that can be booked—library collection material, as well as rooms, computers, room keys, and audiovisual or other equipment. A bibliographic and item record are created for each piece in the catalog database so that the system can create and store a booking. For example, for the booking of multiple projectors or audio equipment each piece needs a record. Library staff can use the booking module to make bookings on request for patrons, and some systems offer options for self-booking by patrons of library-specified material.

CIRCULATION STATISTICS

For reporting purposes, library managers need to know how the collection is used. The library system records daily circulation usage and collates the data into a statistics file that cumulates over a period of time set by the system. Circulation statistics include the number of items borrowed, by which patrons, and from which parts of the collection. Statistical reports can be generated as needed and compared to loan statistics over different time periods.

REVIEW QUESTIONS

1. How does a circulation system determine a loan period when it checks an item out?
2. Describe the difference between barcodes and RFID tags.
3. What is the function of an item or holding record in a circulation system?
4. Explain the difference between holds and bookings.

Chapter 7

Serials

TERMINOLOGY

aggregator: Vendor or distributor that licenses and provides access to multiple electronic resources, such as full-text journals and online databases.

authentication: Verification that a user belongs to an institution to enable access to electronic resources.

binding: Process to bind the individual issues of a serial volume into one single volume.

chronology: Description of the dates of publication of serial issues, e.g., day, month and year; season and year.

e-checkin: Checking in of serial issues using an electronic packing slip, which is a file of issue information that automatically updates checkin records and cards.

e-journal, electronic journal: A journal or serial published online, via the Internet.

electronic resource management: A software product that stores and tracks electronic resource data such as licensing, access, financial information, and contact details.

enumeration: Description of the numbering and parts that make up a serial, e.g., volume and issue, number or part.

frequency: Description of the number of times a serial is issued, e.g., daily, weekly, three times a week, monthly, quarterly, annual.

holdings: Details of a library's collection of a serial title, indicating starting date, gaps in the holdings, or ending date.

ISSN (International Standard Serial Number): a unique number allocated to a serial when published; EISSN is used for electronic serials.

OpenURL: A standard that enables online linking from a journal citation, a bibliographic record, or a catalog search to full texts and other electronic resources.

routee: Name of a person on a serial ROUTING list.

routing: The distribution of serial issues to staff before making the issues available library patrons.

serials checkin: A process that records the receipt of individual serial issues.

SFX: A software product that enables linking among multiple online resources using the OpenURL standard.

SICI (Serial Item and Contribution Identifier Standard): An identifying number stored in a barcode on a serial cover, mostly with academic serial titles; incorporates the ISSN, volume, and issue details.

UPC (Universal Product Code): Barcode number on mass market magazines; does not include the ISSN.

SERIALS CONTROL

Management of print serials in libraries involves tracking the receipt and movement of individual serial issues. Serials modules in an integrated library system enable staff to keep detailed records of issues received, and to follow up on issues not received. Serials records display through the OPAC where library patrons can view information such as:

- dates received
- expected dates
- not received and reasons
- missing issues
- not held by the library
- location

E-journals are accessible from the online catalog via the Internet. A library does not need to keep track of the arrival and whereabouts of issues of e-journals in the same way it does for printed serials. However, electronic journal usage involves different management issues—licensing and subscriptions, availability and access, authentication, and maintaining electronic holdings details.

TYPES OF SERIALS

A serial is defined as an ongoing or continuing publication that appears in successive parts at regular or irregular intervals, for example, annually, monthly, weekly, daily, and is intended to be published indefinitely. Examples of serials are newspapers, magazines, journals, annual reports, handbooks or calendars, and updates to loose-leaf publications.

Serials are published in a range of formats—on paper, microfilm or microfiche (cumulations of newspapers and journal indexes), and electronically (e-journals). Some serials come in more than one format. For example, some journals are published in paper as well as electronic format. A library may subscribe to a journal in both print and electronic formats, or only one. Some journals published electronically are only accessible via the Internet, for example, D-*Lib Magazine* <http://www.dlib.org>, or *Salon.com* <http://salon.com>.

A standing order is a hybrid monograph and serial publication. It refers to items published regularly or irregularly, whereby each item is a separate publication and is cataloged as a monograph. Libraries take on standing orders to receive each item as it is published, similar to a serial subscription. An example is regional travel guides, such as *Fodor's,* which are updated and republished at different intervals. Serials management modules record the publication and receipt of standing orders, and facilitate claiming of overdue publications.

SERIAL RECORDS

In an integrated library system a bibliographic record exists in the catalog for each serial title held by the library. The bibliographic record describes serial publication details, and if it is electronic, includes the URL or Internet address. In the serials module a checkin record attaches or links to each bibliographic record. The serials checkin record contains information about the subscription — price, vendor—as well as statements of the library's holdings. Multiple checkin records representing separate subscriptions, library locations, or formats may link to one bibliographic record. The system assigns a unique record number to each checkin record.

The serials checkin record includes fixed fields containing coded data used for processing and statistical purposes. Variable-length fields contain free-text data such as local processing and maintenance, history notes, call numbers, and holdings statements. Figure 7.1 shows a checkin record with fixed fields and variable-length holdings fields.

Holdings Statements

A serial's holdings statement indicates the dates and volumes held by a library for a specific copy of the serial. The bibliographic record describes the frequency of a serial, and its starting date and volume information, but data reflecting the varying holdings for each subscription are stored in holdings statements in checkin records.

Libraries can create holdings statements as either MARC or non-MARC fields. MARC statements are formatted to follow a specific style, for example, the MARC 21 holdings format includes paired MARC fields to indicate chronology and enumeration (863-865) and corresponding captions and patterns (fields 853-855). Free-text holdings information is stored in fields 866-868. Non-MARC statements are free text and the library determines the format of data. Both MARC and non-MARC statements translate to a single statement in the online OPAC.

Figure 7.1 shows examples of MARC 21 formatted holdings statements in a serials checkin record. The captions (v., no., (year)) in field 853 pair with the numbers in field 863 to represent the chronology and enumeration of the serial issues. The data match on subfields |a, |b, |i in each field. In the 853 field (year) in parentheses indicates that

Record number: 1452637

Location: lvl6	Copies: 1	Routing: yes	Vendor: ABC
Created: 12-12-2005		Modified: 01-02-2006	

853	$8 1 $a v. $b no. $i (year)	*Captions and pattern basic bibliographic unit*
854	$8 1 $a v.	*Captions and pattern supplementary material*
863	$8 1.1$a1-$b1-$i2001-	*Enumeration and chronology basic bibliographic unit*
864	$8 1 $a1-3	*Enumeration and chronology supplementary material*

Predicted issues for bibliographic record   ***Australian Library Journal:***

Enumeration and chronology	Expected date	Received date
v.54:no.1 (Feb 2005)	Feb 20, 2005	Feb 28, 2005
v.54:no.2 (May 2005)	May 20, 2005	June 1, 2005
v.54:no.3 (Aug 2005)	Aug 20, 2005	
v.54:no.4 (Nov 2005)	Nov 20, 2005	
v.55:no.1 (Feb 2005)	Feb 20, 2005	
v.5 5:no.2 (May 2005)	May 20, 2005	
v.55:no.3 (Aug 2005)	Aug 20, 2005	
v 55:no 4 (Nov 2005)	Nov 20 2005	

FIGURE 7.1. Serials checkin record showing fixed fields, MARC holdings fields, and checkin grid.

the word year does not display in the OPAC. In the 863 field the dash in the date 2001- indicates that the serial holding is ongoing. Paired fields 854 and 864 are holdings statements that refer to separately issued supplements.

Figure 7.2 shows an OPAC view of a serial record. The descriptive holding data stored in the bibliographic MARC field 362 indicate that the journal started publication with volume 1, number 1 in July 1951 (Vol.1, no. 1, (July 1951) –). The dash indicates that the library's subscription is still ongoing. The library has two copies in different locations, and the holdings statements for both locations are displayed in the two LIB HAS fields taken from two separate checkin records.

```
001     379892
008     890501c19519999xna            uO       eng   nas
010     |o379892
022     0004-9670
043     u-at---
082  00 020.5|219
222   4 The Australian library journal
245  14 The Australian library journal
260     Sydney :|bLibrary Association of Australia,|c1951-
362   0 Vol. 1, no. 1 (July 1951)-
500     Description based on: Vol. 1 (1951)
650  00 Libraries|xPeriodicals
650  00 Libraries|zAustralia|xPeriodicals
650  00 Library science|xPeriodicals
710   2 Library Association of Australia
```

Location	CITY CAMPUS
LIB. HAS	Vol. 1 (1951) +
Call No.	020.5/11
Latest Received:	November 2003 v.52 no.4
Location	KURING-GAI CAMPUS
LIB. HAS	Vol. 1 (1951)-v.46, no.2 (1997)
Call No.	020.5 AUS 1

FIGURE 7.2. Public view of a serial bibliographic MARC record, with individual location details.

Predicting Serial Issues

When creating checkin records, library personnel analyzes the serial and input frequency, chronology, and enumeration data for each title. These terms are defined as follows.

- *Frequency* refers to the pattern of publication—annual, quarterly, monthly, bimonthly, weekly, three times a month, five times a week, daily, or irregular.
- *Chronology* describes the dates of publication of the serial title, in months, weeks, days, or years.
- *Enumeration* is the description of how issues are numbered, for example, volume and number, part, or issue. The levels of

enumeration refer to the number of serial parts issued and how they are grouped. For example, a serial issued in volumes and numbers has two levels of enumeration. A serial issued only with numbering, and no volumes, has one level of enumeration. A serial with no numbering has zero levels of enumeration, using only chronology or dates to identify each issue.

Using frequency, chronology, and enumeration the serials module predicts expected dates, cover dates, and numbering. These data are stored in a format (similar to a physical card) representing each issue in boxes or lines, as shown in Figure 7.3. Serials modules accommodate many variations in frequency, chronology and enumeration.

Figure 7.3 displays issue information for a serial with a quarterly frequency.

The boxes indicate the following statuses:

- BOUND: issues received and bound into one annual volume box for 1994–2002
- ARRIVED: quarterly issues received for 2003
- EXPECTED: predicted quarterly issues for 2004 and Feb 2005 with expected arrival dates

1994 BOUND on 21-06-95 43	1995 BOUND on 11-02-97 44	1996 BOUND on 20-03-97 45	1997 BOUND on 20-07-99 46	1998 BOUND on 20-07-99 47	1999 BOUND on 16-10-00 48
2000 BOUND on 25-07-01 49	2001 BOUND on 31-07-02 50	2002 BOUND on 16-10-03 51	Feb 2003 ARRIVED on 14-04-03 52:1	May 2003 ARRIVED on 16-07-03 52:2	Aug 2003 ARRIVED on 05-09-03 52:3
Nov 2003 ARRIVED on 13-11-03 52:4	Feb 2004 EXPECTED on 07-03-04 53:1	May 2004 EXPECTED on 07-06-04 53:2	Aug 2004 EXPECTED on 07-09-04 53:3	Nov 2004 EXPECTED on 07-12-04 53:4	Feb 2005 EXPECTED on 07-03-05 54:1

FIGURE 7.3. Public view of issue boxes for an individual serial.

The chronology is indicated for each box by:

- the *month* and *year* of the cover date
- the *year* for bound volumes

The enumeration is indicated by the single number (51) for bound volumes and by two levels for arrived and received issues in the format *volume: issue* (54:1).

Activity dates are shown for:

- date Bound
- date Arrived (received)
- date Expected

In addition to entries for individual serial issues, entries for supplements and indexes are included in checkin cards. A checkin card also stores parameters for claiming and binding of serials.

CHECKING IN SERIALS

As each issue of a serial is received in the library, serials staff login to the serials system module to check in the issue. The first step is to search the catalog database to retrieve the serial's bibliographic and attached checkin records. Indexes to search by include title, ISSN, SICI, or UPC numbers, corporate author, or system record number. SICI and UPC numbers stored in a barcode are placed on the front or back cover of some serials. Barcodes can be scanned with a reader or wand to retrieve the bibliographic record from the database without keying in data.

The next step is to open the checkin record and use the checkin function to record receipt of the issue. The serials system automatically inserts the date received, and changes the status of the issue to indicate it has arrived. Other status labels such as Not Published, Out of Print, Unavailable, Missing, and Removed describe situations when serial issues do not arrive or are no longer in the library. Additional notes or messages convey further information about a serial subscription.

Printing Labels

In some systems, as issues are checked in, spine and cover labels are printed either one at a time, or placed in a batch for printing at a later date. The library specifies label formats and the details to print for different serials, such as title, location, call number. For library systems that do not include label printing libraries use OCLC cataloging label printing program, import system call number data into separate label printing software, or manually create labels.

Circulating Serials

If the library allows serial issues to circulate, an item record is created for issues to store circulation data. Depending on the workflow of the library, the item record is created by serials staff at the time of checkin, or later by cataloging staff. As soon as the item, checkin and bibliographic records are in the system the serial issue can circulate.

Electronic Checkin

Some library systems have a function that enables print and electronic serials to be checked in electronically in batches, known as e-checkin. A serials vendor uploads an electronic packing slip (EPS) file to the library system that lists the specific issues being sent or updated for e-journals. The library uses the Serials module to process the EPS file. The system uses the data to update appropriate checkin cards and holdings statements and to indicate that an issue has arrived. The e-checkin process generates item records and labels as needed.

CLAIMING

Hundreds and thousands of serials are sent by publishers, vendors, or distributors to just as many libraries on a regular basis. Most issues arrive, but some go missing and do not arrive, or are delayed in publication and delivery. Serials modules incorporate claiming functionality to notify vendors if issues are not received by the library.

The claiming module process identifies late issues, marks them to be claimed, and sends details to the vendor. A serial claim can be either for an individual title, or multiple titles on a systematic basis. Individual title claiming occurs if staff discover from library users or other staff that an issue is late. Serials staff retrieve the serials record from the database, check the dates, and mark the late issue for claiming. With systematic claiming, using library-specified criteria, the system retrieves and displays checkin records for staff to review and mark for claiming if appropriate. Libraries define the criteria for claiming for each title, such as the number of days to wait after the expected date before claiming.

Staff can submit claims for late issues to a vendor in several ways, depending on the library system and the serial vendor's capabilities:

- printed forms are mailed
- claims are sent via e-mail or EDI (Electronic Data Interchange)
- staff can phone vendor directly
- vendors may offer claiming functionality on their Web sites

If claiming occurs within the serial module's claiming procedure, the system makes a note in the checkin record of the date claimed, and keeps track of the number of times the issue has been claimed.

BINDING

For serials that a library wants to keep and not discard, a complete set of received issues may be bound into one or two volumes. Many libraries send serials to specialized bindery services.

The serials module has options to indicate binding information and status for individual titles. Similar to the claiming process, binding is achieved on a title-by-title basis, or systematically, using parameters that library staff set for each title added to the system. The binding parameters indicate:

- how many issues should be bound together into one volume
- how many more subsequent issues to receive before issues are sent to binding (binding delay)
- whether or not to bind indexes and supplements
- details about the binding cover color and title lettering and font

Using the serials module, library staff can identify titles ready for binding and update the checkin cards to reflect the change. When instructed by staff, the system marks issues for binding and changes the status to indicate that the issues are waiting to be sent to the binder, or are at the binder. As items return from the bindery, they are checked in, and the status changes to BOUND. Separate issue boxes can collapse into one Bound box for a volume (see Figure 7.3), or stay as separate boxes. The system can update MARC 21 holdings statements automatically to reflect the individual bound volume holdings, if required. Changes in status and holdings display immediately in OPAC.

ROUTING

Some libraries physically circulate serial titles to staff or departments as soon as issues arrive, as a preview service for staff. For example, library science journals may circulate among library staff, or, in a special library, core subject journals circulate to key staff in the organization. This procedure is called routing. The issues do not circulate via the circulation system. Instead, a list of staff names attached to the cover of the serial controls the routing. Individual staff members manually cross off their names from the routing list when they have read the routed issues.

A serials module may include a routing function to record the names of staff and the serial titles they want to have routed to them. When an issue is checked in, the system generates a printed list of names, known as routees, from the routing information stored with the serial title. For e-journals that do not exist in print format, an e-mail message is sent to routees, informing them that a new issue has been published and providing a linked, active URL Web address.

ELECTRONIC SERIALS MANAGEMENT

Electronic serials issues are not checked in because they do not arrive physically in a library, and generally do not have to be tracked for nondelivery and claiming. Yet there are other issues relevant to the management of electronic serials.

Updating Electronic Holdings

Holdings statements that describe the starting dates and gaps in library holdings for electronic serial titles can be updated from a file. The library imports or downloads a formatted file of updated holdings from a supplying vendor and the system locates and updates the holdings statements for records in the file.

Electronic Resource Management

Electronic resources have licensing and subscription data that libraries need to track and maintain. A library may have multiple subscriptions with electronic journal providers, and for each title licenses, subscriptions, and usage must be tracked. Some library systems include functionality to manage electronic resource licensing details. For example, Figure 7.4 shows online catalog entries for the journal *Online* indicating its full text is available electronically from several resources. The data in Figure 7.4 show:

- the library has a license or subscription with serials aggregators Proquest Computing, ABI Inform Global, and Academic Research Library to provide full texts of this journal
- access to the journal is from the hyperlink Electronic Version, maintained by a MARC 856 field containing the URL or Internet address in the bibliographic record
- access to the electronic journal is also available by selecting the SFX button (see as follows)

FIGURE 7.4. An OPAC search result showing full text providers for the electronic version of the journal *Online.*

Linking Software

OpenURL is a National Information Standards Organization (NISO) standard that specifies how to create links from a journal citation or bibliographic serial record to a range of full text and other Internet-based resources. In Figure 7.5 SFX software uses OpenURL to link from the SFX buttons in Figure 7.4. The SFX window displays the following:

- four electronic journal aggregators that provide full text journals (select the title)
- options to view a specific volume and issue by entering enumeration details. By contrast, in Figure 7.4, the link Electronic Version will lead to a display of all volumes and issues for the title.

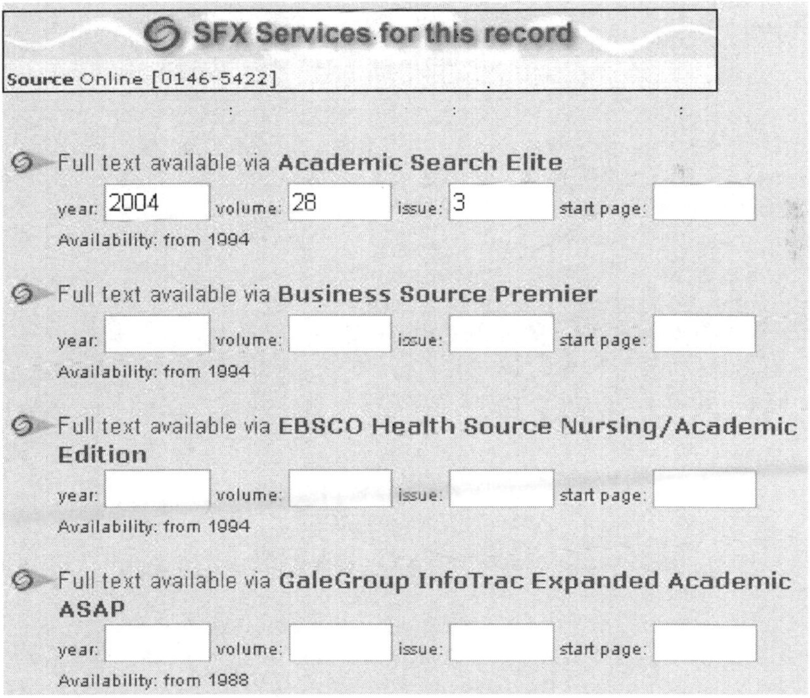

FIGURE 7.5. SFX OpenURL links to full text resources for the journal *Online*.

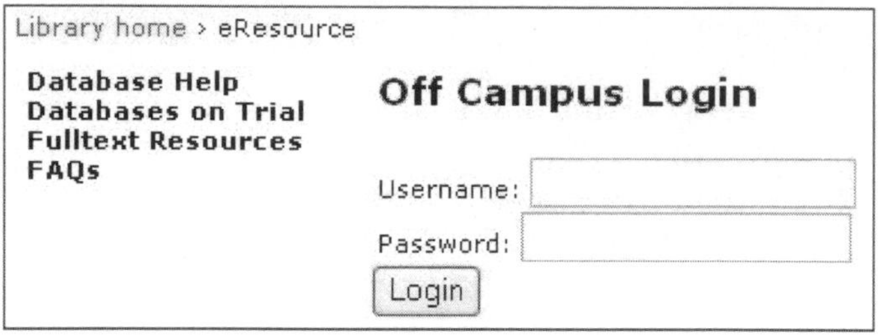

FIGURE 7.6. Authentication window for remote access to online resources.

Libraries can customize OpenURL software settings to determine options that display in the linked window shown in Figure 7.5. Chapter 8 and 10 further discuss the linking of electronic resources.

Authentication

To fulfill licensing requirements, libraries must verify that users of electronic resources are library patrons. On-site authentication is managed by supplying vendors with Internet address ranges of library or organizational computers. Remote or off-site access requires the verification of patrons before connection to a full-text electronic journal or online database. Some products authenticate users against the circulation patron database. Other options integrate stand-alone products into the library system or use a library's parent institution authentication process, such as a campus directory service.

After successful verification, the link to the electronic resource is completed and patrons can access the resource. Figure 7.6 shows a typical authentication window.

REVIEW QUESTIONS

1. Explain the difference between a checkin record and a bibliographic record.
2. What does the enumeration describe about a serial?
3. Name three methods for claiming late serial issues.
4. What are two of the ways that electronic resources can be managed?

Chapter 8

The Online Public Access Catalog

TERMINOLOGY

Boolean operators: Logical connectors that combine words in a KEYWORD SEARCH.

browse list: Result of a catalog search listing multiple records.

digital library: A collection of material that is digitized for online access.

direct hit: Result of a catalog search that finds a single record or item.

federated searching: The ability to search simultaneously across multiple electronic resources; also called METASEARCHING.

firewall: Software that blocks connections to and from a computer server.

HTML (hypertext markup language): Language that describes the display of data on the World Wide Web.

HTTP (hypertext transfer protocol): The technical standard for transferring Web pages across the Internet.

hybrid library: A library collection that combines material in print and digital formats.

hypertext: Method of navigating between documents on the World Wide Web using links embedded in documents.

keyword search: Retrieval from databases using words that appear anywhere in a stored record or text.

metadata: Data that describe documents or objects; used for retrieval of records from an online system.

metasearching: See FEDERATED SEARCHING.

OPAC (Online Public Access Catalog): Public view of an online library catalog; also called PAC (Public Access Catalog).

 OpenURL: A standard that enables linking from a journal citation or bibliographic record to a range of full text and other Internet resources.

 phrase searching: Retrieval of records by the first words in indexed fields such as title, author, or subject.

portal: A gateway to information resources offered from the OPAC.

SGML (standard generalized markup language): A method of marking text for publishing.

Shibboleth: An open, standards-based solution to the exchange of information about users in a secure and privacy-preserving manner.

URL (uniform resource locator): A Web page address on the Internet.

XML (extensible markup language): a markup language that describes a wide range of electronic documents; a subset of SGML.

Web OPAC: An online public access catalog that displays on the World Wide Web.

THE WEB OPAC

The Online Public Access Catalog (OPAC) is the integrated library system's window to a world of users. Using the World Wide Web protocol, OPACs are accessible on the Internet twenty-four hours a day from anywhere in the world. A Web OPAC offers patrons a myriad of online resources to access from within a library, from a home computer, or any remote Internet connection. As electronic publishing and digital collections grow, libraries use the Web OPAC to expand and offer hybrid collections combining print and electronic or digital resources. *LibDex, the Worldwide Index of Library Catalogs* <http:// www.libdex.com/> lists over 18,000 public online catalogs; many more catalogs are not available publicly.

A successful Web OPAC depends on two key elements: good interface and navigation design, and appropriate indexing and searching capabilities.

Web OPAC Design

The Web OPAC is the primary finding tool for a library's resources. For some people it may be their only view of the library. As well as linking to the online catalog a library Web page includes information about collection highlights, library hours, news and events, and selected Web resources. A well-designed Web OPAC uses a combination of artistic and technical expertise, and knowledge of the language and capabilities of the Web. The most effective Web pages provide a simple layout with clear navigation paths so that information is easy to find.

HTML

The display of data on the Web is achieved by the use of HTML (hypertext markup language), a simplified version of SGML (standard generalized markup language). Web browser software programs such as Netscape and Internet Explorer interpret and display the HTML in Web pages.

HTML is not a programming language, and it is easy to learn and use. It consists of a set of tags and attributes placed around text for display. Only the text and files within the tags are seen in the Web. Display elements controlled by HTML are:

- color and size of textual fonts
- background colors and designs

- hypertext links to other pages, Web sites, or files
- location of image or graphical files
- layout, spacing and location of text, images and files

You can view the HTML source of a Web page at any time to see how it was put together by selecting the Web browser toolbar option View | Source. Figure 8.1 shows a Web OPAC and a section of its HTML source code.

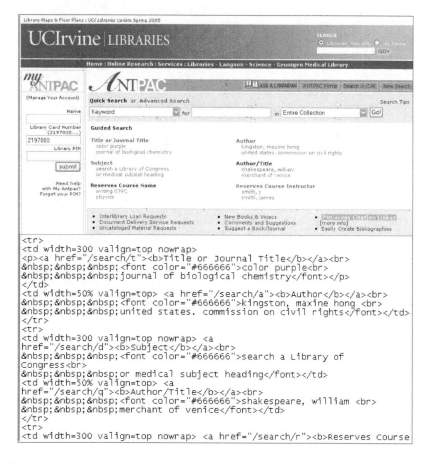

FIGURE 8.1. Search menu and section of the HTML source from ANTPAC, the University of California Irvine Library Web OPAC. Reprinted with permission of University of California Irvine.

Most Web designers use HTML editing programs to create Web pages. For more information about HTML see the section on Creating Content for the World Wide Web in Chapter 11.

Customizing the Web OPAC

A standard or "out-of-the-box" series of Web pages comes installed with an integrated library system. Libraries customize the Web OPAC pages, incorporating local design, images, logos, and content. After system installation, ongoing maintenance of the Web OPAC is the library's responsibility.

A Web OPAC has two types of HTML pages, static and dynamic. Static pages are informational pages whose content changes only when the library edits them. The opening Web page offering catalog search options in Figure 8.1 is a library-customized page. It includes links to local related information such as new books and videos.

By contrast, because the content of each search query varies, Web OPAC search results are dynamic. When the library system delivers a search result it creates a new Web page each time, using a combination of system formatting and display options set by the library. The format of search results is the same, but their content changes dynamically. Figure 8.2 shows a search result listing of records that satisfy a search query for titles containing *xml*. If a search were for titles containing *HTML* the resulting content would be different and the catalog would generate a new page. To achieve this, the formatting and specifications are set within the system.

Public View

Online library catalogs provide different record displays for staff and public. The OPAC view of a bibliographic record has less detail and is formatted differently from the record that displays for staff within the system. Selected fields display and field labels use more friendly, less technical language. For example, MARC tag 260 represents the Imprint field, but library users may not be familiar with this term, so the OPAC label is Published, Publisher, or Publication. Links

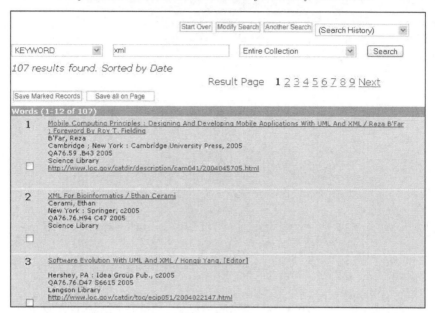

FIGURE 8.2. Web OPAC dynamic keyword search result page.

from a brief display to full and MARC bibliographic records are optional. Figure 8.3 shows the public view of a bibliographic record with a choice of other display formats—Catalog card (brief), Citation, MARC tags.

Figure 8.4 shows the holdings and loan information from the record in Figure 8.3. Item data that display are location, local call number, and type of loan.

SEARCHING AND INDEXING

The primary function of the online library catalog is to enable library users to search, find, retrieve, and locate resources within and outside the library. Following are some options the library system can provide.

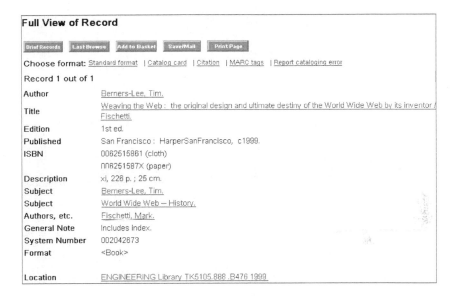

FIGURE 8.3. Full view of an OPAC catalog record.

Indexing

When installing an online system, a library makes indexing decisions at the outset:

- the indexes needed as search or access points
- fields and parts of fields to be included or excluded from indexes
- indexes that will be offered to the public

The system indexes record fields according to the rules set by the library and create searchable indexes. When a library user searches an index, for example, by author name, the system finds the name in the author index, and displays all records linked to the entry.

Figure 8.1 shows six indexes or search points: author, title, subject, keyword, author/title, reserves course name, and reserves course instructor. On the search page, hypertext links point back to the indexes in the catalog database. As well as the indexes in Figure 8.1, libraries can add links for journal title, call numbers, ISBN, ISSN, or other numbers if the indexes exist in the system.

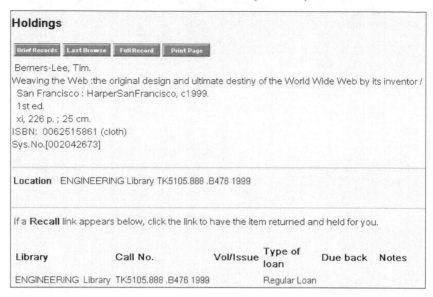

Holdings

[Brief Records] [Last Browse] [Full Record] [Print Page]

Berners-Lee, Tim.
Weaving the Web :the original design and ultimate destiny of the World Wide Web by its inventor /
San Francisco : HarperSanFrancisco, c1999.
1st ed.
xi, 226 p. ; 25 cm.
ISBN: 0062515861 (cloth)
Sys.No.[002042673]

Location ENGINEERING Library TK5105.888 .B476 1999

If a **Recall** link appears below, click the link to have the item returned and held for you.

Library	Call No.	Vol/Issue	Type of loan	Due back	Notes
ENGINEERING Library TK5105.888 .B476 1999			Regular Loan		

FIGURE 8.4. Holdings information for the record shown in Figure 8.3.

Searching the OPAC

Online public access catalogs offer both phrase and keyword searching.

Phrase Searching

A phrase search looks in the selected index for words in the order they appear in the record, i.e., as strings of words.

Author names are stored in the author phrase index in the format last name, first name, e.g., *Berners-Lee, Tim.* An author phrase search for *Berners-Lee* looks for entries beginning with that name.

An advantage of phrase searching is that you need only enter the first few words of a field and the system retrieves all entries beginning with your search terms. The result is a browse list, from which you select titles to view. If a phrase search matches an indexed field exactly, the system returns just that one record. This is referred to as a direct hit, as distinct from a browse list result.

Figure 8.5 shows a drop-down menu of multiple phrase search options for indexes. In the background is a browse list resulting from a search for titles beginning with *Weaving the web*. Libraries can specify the indexes that are included in the drop-down search menu.

In some OPACs titles beginning with initial articles such as *a, an, the, los,* or *un* are filed or indexed under the next word following the initial article, so that multiple titles are not grouped under the common initial articles. This is achieved by adding an instruction to the MARC title field indicating the number of nonfiling characters (initial characters) to be skipped for indexing purposes. Although initial articles are present in the title in the bibliographic record, you do not need to enter them in a search.

For example, A title beginning *The Web of Life* has a four character skip (made up of three characters in *The* and one following space).

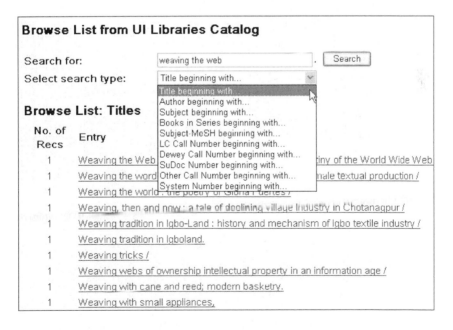

FIGURE 8.5. Phrase search options in different fields in a Web OPAC.

The MARC title field 245 includes the instruction to skip four characters in the second indicator: *245 14 The web of life.*

Reading the indicator in the MARC record, the system skips the initial article *The* and following space, filing the title under the next word, *Web.* The catalog then ignores the initial article if patrons include it in their search.

Library systems that do not use the skip feature provide instructions to patrons to omit initial articles.

 Keyword Searching

Keyword searching uses a separate keyword index made up of words from multiple bibliographic fields. Libraries specify the fields and subfields to add to a keyword index and each word is listed separately in the index. A keyword search retrieves records containing the search words wherever they appear in a field, not just at the beginning as with phrase searching. Searching within separate keyword indexes, such as title, author, and subject, provides more specific results.

Boolean and proximity operators combine multiple search terms in a keyword search. Boolean operators AND, OR, NOT, specify that:

- words joined by AND must occur in the same record
- any or all of the words joined by OR can occur in the same record
- words following NOT must not occur, and records with that word are excluded

Adjacency operators determine the proximity of keywords to each other, a closer relationship than that specified by AND, the Boolean operator. Words can occur either as a phrase or with a number of words between the search keywords. For more information on Boolean and proximity search operators see the section on Online Searching Skills in Chapter 11.

Online catalogs provide extended keyword search options from an Advanced Search screen such as that in Figure 8.6.

1. Each of the three Search for: boxes can link to another using one of the Boolean operators AND, OR, NOT.

2. Specify within each search box if words should be searched *as a phrase* (using *adjacent*), *all of these* words (using AND), or *any of these* words (using OR)
3. For each search box choose an index to search within, for example, Keywords (anywhere)
4. Specify the number of records to display on each page

Record Display and Output Options

Libraries can determine the record display of search results. For example, from a direct hit result, a search that finds one record, the display is in full or brief format, showing fields specified by the library. A browse list of multiple records displays in brief, with fields such as author and title, date, location, format, or medium (e.g., book, DVD, online).

Search screens offer options to sort results, by date, alphabetical, or relevance to the searched topic (based on whether search words appear in the title or elsewhere in a record).

Options for outputting search results include printing, downloading to a local computer drive or network drive, or e-mailing. Patrons choose the output format of records determined by the library—brief, full, MARC, or reference management software such as EndNote or Procite.

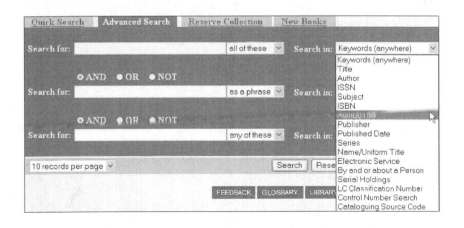

FIGURE 8.6. Advanced keyword search options in a Web OPAC.

PORTALS: LINKING BEYOND THE OPAC

A library portal offers a gateway from the Web OPAC to digital resources, as well as *my-space,* a personal space for library patrons to view borrowing records, store search strategies and preferred database resources.

Through a portal, patrons can link to other library catalogs, subject-grouped Web sites, indexing and abstracting databases, and full texts of electronic journals to which libraries subscribe. Searching for information has become richer, but also more complex. Two options for streamlining access to multiple resources are federated searching across resources and OpenURL linking from citations to selected resources, including journal full texts.

Federated Searching

Libraries subscribe to specialized databases, citation databases, digital collections, and full texts of journals. Web OPACs link to Web search engines and directories such as Google or Yahoo. Federated searching (metasearching or broadcast searching) enables simultaneous searching across a range of online resources. One can select resources, enter search words, and receive results from multiple resources. If more than one resource finds the same records, the program removes duplicate records before delivering the results to the screen (known as de-duping). A progress report displays for each resource, advising the number of results found, and the time remaining before each displays its results. The advantage of federated searching is that you do not need to repeat the search terms for each database selected.

Figure 8.7 shows the Cleveland Public Library's federated search, OneSearch, offering a number of options:

- select the alphabetical list of databases, or
- search the most popular databases and
- include the library catalog in the search, or
- select a database by format or subject area.

Many library vendors have incorporated metasearch technology into their systems. Libraries can purchase and install stand-alone metasearch products separately from the integrated library management system.

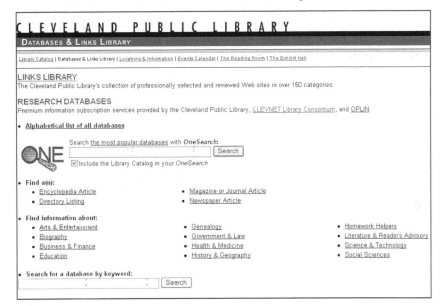

FIGURE 8.7. OneSearch, the Cleveland Public Library's federated search. Reprinted with permission by the Cleveland Public Library.

 ## *Open URL Linking*

OpenURL linking technology provides direct links from journal citations and catalog search results to full text and other digital resources. It differs from metasearching in that the search begins in a single resource such as the OPAC or a citation database. Then, by selecting a button or link in the search result, a separate window provides a choice of links to full-text databases or subject-related resources. Chapters 7 and 10 include examples of OpenURL linking.

Z39.50

The information retrieval standard Z39.50 enables the searching of online library catalogs and vendor databases from within an online catalog. Libraries create Z39.50 database links that enable patrons to search other catalogs using their library OPAC search interface. The Z39.50 standard has been largely superseded by the use of direct Web hypertext links.

My Library

Many Web sites offer a space to store personal information. On Web OPACs it is called My Library, My Record, or My Account. It allows patrons to login to their personal record to view checkouts and fines, renew material, cancel holds, and update or modify personal information. Patrons can also store database searches and selected resources in this personal space.

SECURITY AND ACCESS

As library catalogs extend across the Internet and the World Wide Web, system and Web servers need protection from hackers, spammers, and viruses. Integrated library systems have built-in security measures to prevent unauthorized access. In many organizations local network controls are applied to the library system, such as placing the server behind a firewall, software that prevents access from outside users. Library staff have to work with technology managers to open ports or points of access to enable system functionality and connections to external resources.

Authentication

The Web OPAC is open to the whole world, but a library's links to subscribed databases must, in terms of vendor license agreements, be limited to registered library users. To achieve this, libraries distribute database usernames and passwords. In a small, controllable environment this can work. But for large organizations in which the user community is less easily defined, libraries control access through authentication or verification methods such as:

- IP address—limiting access to databases to computers from a specified range of IP (Internet Protocol) addresses within a library or institution
- Remote patron verification—off-site library users enter their library card or ID details to be verified in a patron database
- Authentication using directory services such as LDAP (Lightweight Directory Access Protocol) or Shibboleth.

DIGITAL LIBRARIES

A digital library is a collection of digitized material that has been scanned, copied, converted to a graphical file format, or photographed with a digital camera. The content of digital libraries is stored on Internet servers and is accessible electronically. Libraries provide digital collections for a number of reasons: to preserve fragile and valuable material; to extend access to material beyond a library building; and increasingly, to incorporate data that are created digitally ("born digital") into collections. Some public digital libraries are the California Digital Library <http://www.cdlib.org/>, the Albert Einstein Archives <http://albert-einstein.org/>, which contain Einstein's letters, manuscripts and diaries, and the Colorado Digitization Program <http://cdpheritage.org/> of historical photographs.

Standards for describing digital library collections expand on the MARC format used in bibliographic cataloging. A popular format is XML (extensible markup language), a simplified version of the publishing markup language SGML. XML is an open, flexible standard that enables descriptions of different formats to suit a user community. Some examples of XML schemes are EAD (Encoded Archival Description) which describes archival finding aids, and METS, the Metadata Encoding and Transmission Standard. For more information on using XML see Creating Content for the World Wide Web in Chapter 11.

Digital Media

Integrated library systems include tools to store and manage digital content such as text, images, video, and audio. Within these modules staff can upload media files to the catalog and link them to bibliographic records. Patrons can search for digital media in the online catalog using both keyword and phrase search techniques.

Figure 8.8 shows a bibliographic record on the Academy of Natural Sciences of Philadelphia, Ewell Sale Stewart Library Web OPAC <http://www.acnatsci.org/library/>. Users can select a thumbnail image to display the full image. This is an example of a hybrid library: a library that combines digital and print material.

Library system digital modules also manage digital rights: the description, identification, protection, monitoring, and tracking of

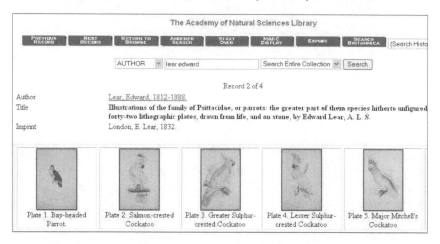

FIGURE 8.8. Thumbnails of images stored in a bibliographic record in the Academy of Natural Sciences of Philadelphia, Ewell Sale Stewart Library catalog. Reprinted with permission by Ewell Sale Stewart Library.

material. Reproduction and use of digital material from Web OPACs and other digital collections is protected under Fair Use guidelines in copyright law. Managing this protection in the open Web environment is a challenge for libraries, and data owners and producers.

The conjunction of the World Wide Web (and the Internet) and the OPAC have pushed library services beyond their traditional offerings. The Web OPAC is the future of libraries.

REVIEW QUESTIONS

1. Name the two types of Web pages that display in a Web OPAC.
2. What is the difference between phrase and keyword searching?
3. What is a hybrid library?
4. Explain the difference between OpenURL linking and federated or metasearching.

Chapter 9

Resource Sharing

TERMINOLOGY

Ariel: The RLG (Research Libraries Group) electronic document delivery system.

ARL: The United States Association of Research Libraries.

consortial borrowing: Schemes and software for interlending among libraries.

consortium: An organization of separate libraries or institutions that share resources, a library system, or develop joint purchasing agreements. Plural is *consortia.*

direct consortial borrowing: The sharing and lending of material among libraries with different systems, using the NCIP protocol.

document delivery: The borrowing of material from sources external to a library that are delivered to local library users; includes delivery of electronic resources. The term is often used interchangeably with INTERLIBRARY LOAN.

holdings: Details of material held by libraries as part of a resource sharing scheme.

ILDS: Interlending and Document Section of the IFLA (International Federation of Library Associations).

(ILL) interlibrary loan: A library procedure that obtains material from a range of sources for use and borrowing by local patrons.

Also the name of the integrated library system module used for this process.

intralibrary loan: The lending of material among branches of a library or libraries that share a library system.

ISO ILL: International standards for interlibrary loan. ISO ILL 10160/10161 are the technical definition of messages and a set of rules specifying how to use the messages to conduct interlibrary loans between different systems.

IPIG: The ILL Protocol Implementors Group.

NCIP: The NISO Z39.83 Circulation Interchange Protocol that enables different automated lending systems to interface.

union catalog, union database: A database of library records accessed by a group of libraries for consortial or universal borrowing; or national and international catalogs of records that provide shared cataloging such as OCLC's World Cat, and the *National Union Catalog* which is the print version published by the Library of Congress.

universal borrowing: Schemes and services for lending material among related libraries; the name of a software product for the same function. *See also* CONSORTIAL BORROWING.

unmediated borrowing: Patron-placed requests for material among consortial libraries that is handled by software, without staff mediation or intervention.

Resource sharing is a broad term that describes the sharing of published material among libraries to extend and enhance local collections. A single library cannot collect everything its patrons may want to read or access, and resource sharing programs extend resources at local, regional, national, and international levels. Resource sharing includes interlibrary loans, the physical interlending of materials among libraries, as well as the electronic delivery of material. This chapter looks at the different programs, standards and automated management products used in libraries.

RESOURCE SHARING STANDARDS

Resource sharing involves the interaction of multiple software products among libraries and incorporates several international standards (and acronyms). The ISO ILL standards are an Open Systems Interconnection suite of Interlibrary Loan (ILL) application standards designed to allow "the interconnection of computer systems from different manufacturers, under different management, of different levels of complexity, and of different ages" (http://www.collections canada.ca/iso/ill/standard.htm). The standards provide support for the control and management of ILL transactions for both lending and borrowing activities. Details are available on the Interlibrary Loan Application Standards Maintenance Agency Web site <http://www. nlc-bnc.ca/iso/ill/main.htm>.

The NCIP NISO Z39.83 Circulation Interchange Protocol is sponsored by the National Information Standards Organization <http:// www.niso.org>. It determines the transactions needed to support patron and item inquiry and update transactions, hold or reserve functions, and checkout, renewal, and check-in among independent library systems. It also supports the circulation of printed and electronic materials and facilitates direct patron borrowing, remote patron authentication, online payment, and controlled access to electronic documents. NCIP enables library circulation systems to transmit standardized messages to other systems and third-party vendors ensuring that their NCIP-compliant products integrate with automated systems.

IPIG, the ILL Protocol Implementors Group, was established in 1995 by the Association of Research Libraries to encourage the implementation of the ILL ISO standards protocol. IPIG has produced guidelines for ILL product developers, and the IPIG Directory, a proposal to use the international LDAP/X500 directory service for communicating between ILL services and libraries.

INTERLIBRARY LOAN

The interlibrary loan (ILL) is a long-established tradition of sharing resources among libraries, and extending the local collection to support research and other areas of interest of library users. Most libraries have active ILL departments and programs. Libraries can be "net lenders"—lending more than they borrow—often found at national, state, and academic libraries with large collections. Smaller college and public libraries may borrow more than they lend, "net borrowers," but a small library with a specialized collection may be a net lender.

Interlibrary Loan Schemes

Centralized ILL services are based around large online databases of national or specialized material. Libraries use the ILL services to verify, identify, and locate material, and place requests. OCLC provides the largest ILL service in the United States, and uses the OCLC WorldCat database of bibliographic library records. Almost 7,000 libraries worldwide use the OCLC ILL service <http://www.oclc.org/ill>. The US Research Libraries Information Network (RLIN) ILL service from RLG (Research Libraries Group) uses the database of bibliographic records and holdings contributed by RLG members and other research collections <http://www.rlg.org>.

DOCLINE, the U.S. National Library of Medicine's automated interlibrary loan service, provides document delivery of journal material among medical and health science libraries in the United States, Canada, Mexico, and other countries <http://www.nlm.nih.gov/pubs/factsheets/docline.html>.

CISTI, the Canada Institute for Scientific and Technical Information, delivers scientific, technical, medical, and agricultural books, journal articles, conference papers and reports from its own collection and several international science and technology collections <http://cisti-icist.nrc-cnrc.gc.ca/docdel/docdel_e.shtml>.

The British Library Document Supply Centre (BLDSC) manages interlibrary loan requests and lending for the British library community and international libraries <http://www.bl.uk/services/document/dsc.html>. Libraries Australia (previously Kinetica) system uses the National Library of Australia's national database for its interlibrary loan or document delivery scheme <http://librariesaustralia.nla.gov.au/apps/kss>.

Member libraries contribute holdings of material in their collections for interlibrary loan to the ILL service databases. Libraries must be subscribed members of a scheme to borrow, and they receive borrowing credits for contributing bibliographic record holdings. Library staff search ILL databases and place requests for items, lending libraries based on geographical proximity, speed of delivery, and collection specialities. Some ILL services allow library patrons to search and request items directly. The ILL service processes the requests and libraries can track their requests. Most ILL services set a fee for each loan.

Electronic ILL

Ariel developed by the Research Libraries Group (RLG), was one of the first electronic delivery schemes used in libraries. Using Ariel hardware and software, scanned electronic documents are transmitted by either FTP or e-mail to Ariel workstations in other libraries. There they convert into PDF files for delivery to patrons. The CISTI and BLDSC ILL services provide secure electronic desktop document delivery. The service centers deliver materials digitally scanned as PDF documents via the World Wide Web for downloading and viewing through Adobe Acrobat Reader desktop software.

Interlibrary Loans Management

Management of ILL requests includes keeping records of patron ILL requests, tracking their progress with an ILL supplier, and recording the local circulation of returnable ILL items. Many integrated library management systems include an ILL module that allows libraries to keep electronic records and circulate ILL loans within the system. Libraries can purchase separate, stand-alone ILL management products to integrate with an existing system, for example, VDX (Virtual Document eXchange) from Fretwell-Downing, ILLiad from OCLC, RLG ILL Management. A good ILL management system is able to:

- receive ILL requests electronically via the library's Web site;
- generate ILL records from both electronic and print requests;
- send requests to ILL suppliers using e-mail or interface directly with a supplier database;
- interact with the local system patron database and circulation module;

- provide print options for sending requests such as form letters; and
- gather, store, and report statistics on all ILL transactions.

Interlibrary Loan Procedures

Procedures for the use of an automated ILL system are as follows (see Figure 9.1 for a diagrammatic version):

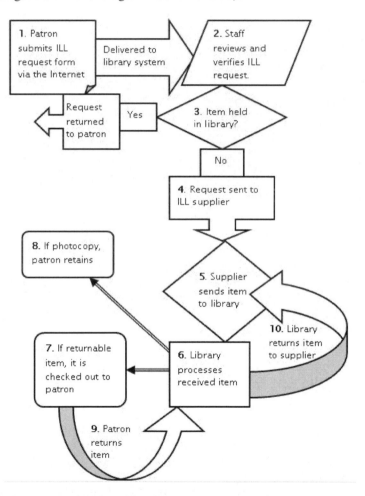

FIGURE 9.1. The local interlibrary loan process.

1. Patrons send ILL requests to their libraries on paper, via e-mail, or using a Web-based form. Figure 9.2 shows a typical Web-based ILL form.
2. The request is converted into an ILL record on the system. Data from e-mail or Web-based requests imported directly into the online ILL record reduce the amount of data input by staff. Some libraries require ILL staff to verify the bibliographic details of requests on other online catalogs or databases to ensure the correct item is requested.
3. The local catalog is checked, and if the requested item is held locally, the request is returned to the patron with advice to consult the local catalog.
4. If the item is to be requested, the most appropriate supplier is selected and the request is sent to the ILL supplier's database via a direct electronic connection, such as an e-mail message, by fax, or mail. The local ILL system records the date the request was received, and the date it was sent to a supplier. The status of a request can be checked anytime on the local system and followed up on the supplier's system. If the item is not available from one supplier, a different supplier is selected.
5. Supplier sends item to the library.
6. When a requested item arrives in the library, the online ILL request is updated by recording the date. If the item is to be returned to the lending library, ILL staff or the library system create an item record to use for checkout in the library's circulation system.
7. The item is checked out to the local patron. ILL staff can track the loan of the item, sending overdue notices as necessary, just as if the item were held in the library's collection. Libraries determine the loan period for returnable items, allowing enough time for processing and delivery to the lending library after a patron has returned the item.
8. Photocopies of book chapters or journal articles, or items in electronic format do not have to be returned to the local or lending library. However, the ILL system still records the arrival date.
9. When returnable items come back to the local library they are checked in and the system removes the loan details from the patron's record.
10. Items are prepared for return to the lending library in the ILL module, recording the return date.

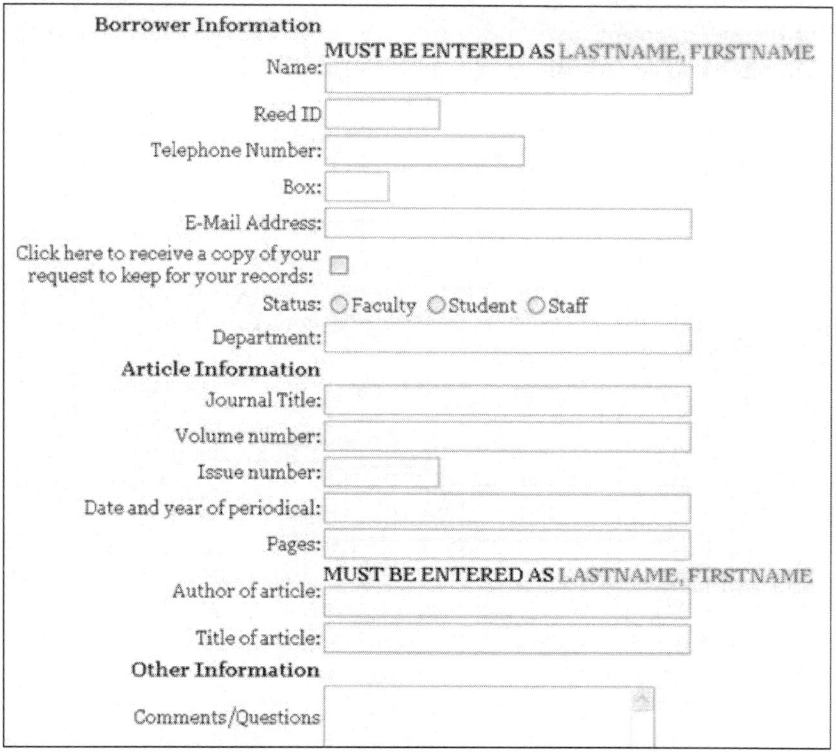

Borrower Information

MUST BE ENTERED AS LASTNAME, FIRSTNAME

Name:

Reed ID

Telephone Number:

Box:

E-Mail Address:

Click here to receive a copy of your request to keep for your records: ☐

Status: ○ Faculty ○ Student ○ Staff

Department:

Article Information

Journal Title:

Volume number:

Issue number:

Date and year of periodical:

Pages:

MUST BE ENTERED AS LASTNAME, FIRSTNAME

Author of article:

Title of article:

Other Information

Comments/Questions

FIGURE 9.2. A Web-based interlibrary loan request form.

Outgoing Interlibrary Loans

Resource sharing is reciprocal, and most libraries both borrow and lend to other libraries under ILL arrangements. ILL lending involves:

- receiving requests from other libraries via e-mail, fax, or mail
- searching the local catalog, identifying and locating copies on the shelves
- checking out items using the local library's circulation system, or delivering electronically to the requesting libraries via Ariel or other document transmission software

Management of lending may be included in ILL software, or developed inhouse. The University of Oregon developed a program called Interlibrary Loan Automated Search And Print (ILL ASAP) that uses XML to automate ILL collection and preparation for delivery. ILL ASAP automatically searches through electronic interlibrary loan requests, and prints request forms sorted by location and call number, complete with availability information, scannable Ariel addresses, shipping labels (if no Ariel address is present), and billing data, customized to the borrowing library or consortium involved (Bannerjee, 2002).

CONSORTIAL BORROWING

Consortia are groups of libraries that work together to share library system databases, make joint system and online database purchases, or to enable reciprocal or universal borrowing. Consortia can be:

- geographically based, for example OhioLINK is a consortium of the libraries of eighty-four Ohio colleges and universities, and the State Library of Ohio;
- subject based, for example, medical or law library consortia; or
- format based, such as CURL, the U.K. Consortium of University Research Libraries that share the COPAC union catalog.

From a resource-sharing point of view, the definition and degree of sharing varies according to the needs of the consortia. If consortia members share a library system and database, individual libraries can borrow one another's materials, and patrons can request items directly from any other library. Such lending and borrowing is sometimes referred to as intralibrary loan. In other situations, consortium libraries may not allow direct borrowing, but use member libraries as the first point of call to supply requests for other material. Figure 9.3 depicts some resource sharing options.

Direct Consortial Borrowing and Union Catalogs

Libraries may contribute their separate online records into a shared central database for the purpose of interlibrary lending and borrowing.

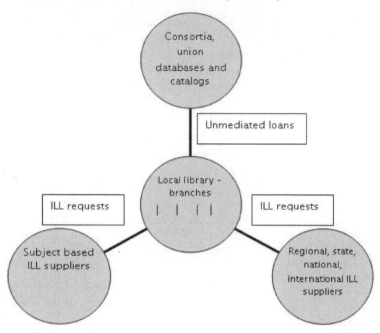

FIGURE 9.3. Resource sharing options.

These joint systems offer a central or union catalogs for patron and staff searching, and unmediated requests (patrons place requests for items through the OPAC, without library staff intervention). Unmediated services expand resources available to library users and reduce the staff time spent on processing ILL requests.

The terminology that describes consortial and union catalog services is somewhat fuzzy and overlapping. Some definitions follow:

1. *Direct consortial borrowing:* Software that enables direct borrowing among libraries with separate systems and databases. The consortia may be geographically based, coming together only for the purpose of sharing resources. Member libraries contribute patron, bibliographic and item data to a central database that is updated in real time to reflect changes to catalog and circulation records. Patrons extend a search from the local OPAC across the central database of material from the contributing

libraries, and, if the software allows, place unmediated requests online for materials. Library staff involvement is only in the collecting and delivery of material. The central circulation system and the lending library's database record immediately display checkouts. If the central software is compliant with the NCIP protocol, it can interact with different integrated library systems. Examples of software that enable such arrangements are the INN-Reach product from Innovative Interfaces, and Dynix Universal Resource Sharing Application (URSA).

2. *Universal borrowing or direct access borrowing:* Universal borrowing also describes a direct consortial borrowing service in which libraries link their databases. The terms universal or direct access borrowing also refer to situations in which patrons can view multiple library holdings online, but physically visit other libraries to borrow materials. Libraries can choose to retain separate bibliographic records in each database, or have them combined at the point of display in the OPAC.

3. *Union catalog or database, virtual catalog:* A collective database that records the holdings of consortia when multiple members share the same integrated system, for example, the University of California Libraries. Union catalog or database refers to the central database of libraries using direct consortial or universal borrowing, but that do not share systems. Union catalogs are also national database interlibrary loan catalogs, such as OCLC's WorldCat, the National Library of Australia's Libraries Australia, and COPAC, the merged online catalogs of twenty-four research libraries in the United Kingdom and Ireland, and subject-based collections.

ILL Developments

IPIG (ILL Protocol Implementors Group) and ARL (Association of Research Libraries) are spearheading developments in ILL requesting and messaging. The two groups are investigating the use of peer-to-peer networking systems to allow libraries to send ILL requests directly to the lending libraries. This would replace the need to use a centralized intermediary ILL service such as OCLC, selecting the best lending library (or more than one) and waiting for the service to send the request on. Other possibilities are unmediated ILL requests, where patrons send their requests directly to ILL suppliers with whom the library has accounts.

REVIEW QUESTIONS

1. List four requirements you would look for in an interlibrary loan management system.
2. Name three worldwide interlibrary loan suppliers.
3. Explain the difference between a consortium and a union database.
4. What are the advantages of unmediated borrowing?

Chapter 10

Information Searching

TERMINOLOGY

abstract: A brief summary of a publication such as a journal article.

abstracting and indexing databases (a&i databases): Online and CD-ROM subject-based databases of citations or references to published material; also referred to as CITATION DATABASES.

aggregators: Vendors that distribute full texts of journals and references electronically.

Boolean operators: Logical connectors used to combine search terms in database searching.

CD-ROM (compact disc read-only memory): A portable disc format that stores reference material such as encyclopedias; *see* CITATION DATABASES.

citation: Data that identify a published article, referring the user to the source of publication; also called a reference.

citation databases: *See* ABSTRACTING AND INDEXING DATABASES.

e-print: An electronic version of a PREPRINT.

electronic journals: Journals published electronically and available on the Internet.

end-user searching: Database search conducted directly by users; compare with MEDIATED SEARCHING.

federated searching: Searching simultaneously across multiple citations or full-text databases, online library catalogs, and Internet search engines; also referred to as METASEARCHING.

full-text databases: Electronic databases that contain full texts of journal articles and other published material.

harvest: A procedure or protocol to gather digital data from multiple databases.

interoperability: The ability of software products to work with different operating systems and integrated library systems.

mediated searching: Online database search conducted by trained library staff; compare with END-USER SEARCHING.

metasearch engine: A tool that searches multiple Web SEARCH ENGINES at once.

metasearching: *See* FEDERATED SEARCHING.

OpenURL linking: The linking of search results and citations to full-text and other online resources.

peer-reviewed: Papers or articles reviewed by peers or colleagues in an author's community before publication in a journal.

preprint: An article that is distributed prior to its official publication in a PEER-REVIEWED journal; if electronic, known as an E-PRINT.

proximity operators: Connecting words that determine the closeness of terms to one another in a database search.

remote access: Online database searching from outside a library or organization's physical space but through the library's Web site and Internet connections.

search engine: A program that uses automated retrieval methods to search through Web sites.

stop words: Common words that are ignored in a database search.

thesaurus: A list of controlled vocabulary or subject headings used for indexing databases.

vendor: A commercial organization providing online, computerized database searching; also called a host.

A citation, index, or abstracting database contains references to material published in journal and newspaper articles, and conference papers. The terms citation, indexing, and abstracting are used interchangeably; the difference between them is whether or not an abstract is included with a citation in a database.

- A *citation* includes the following data: author, title of article, source of publication (journal, newspaper, conference), date (day, month, year), volume and numbering details, and page numbers.
- An *abstracting service* includes a brief abstract or description of the article content, as well as the citation data.

Full text refers to the complete text of an item referred to in a citation. Many online indexing and abstracting services include options to view, read, and download the full text of the item, often linking to a separate service. Online citation, indexing, and abstracting tools locate published material in all subject areas.

TYPES OF DATABASES

Citation Databases

During the 1980s, as publishing and printing procedures became automated, databases of indexed citation data were built. Search programs were written to enable users to search database indexes and retrieve citations or references. Two of the first online databases developed that are still in use today are Medline Plus, the online version of the U.S. National Library of Medicine's printed *Index Medicus* <http://www.nlm.nih.gov>, and ERIC (Educational Resources Information

Center), the U.S. Department of Education's database of education-related documents <http://www.eric.ed.gov/searchdb/index.html>. Both databases are government-funded services that offer free search and delivery of citations and abstracts.

Commercial search services from vendors such as Dialog Information Services, Ovid, and SilverPlatter offer fee-based searching of resources such as *Chemical Abstracts, Science Citation Index, Social Sciences Index, Psychological Abstracts, Physics Abstracts, Humanities Index,* and *Readers' Guide to Periodical Literature.* Libraries pay an annual subscription fee to provide database access for patrons through local network and Internet connections.

The extent of library patron use of online database services varies among libraries. End-user or patron searching is high in academic and public libraries, but lower in special or corporate libraries (law, business, government, management consultants) where library professionals provide mediated searching for staff as part of a research service.

CD-Rom Databases

Databases in CD-ROM format use technology that was developed originally for music CDs (compact discs). CD-ROMs are accessed from individual computers and local-area CD-ROM networks. CD-ROM databases replaced volumes of printed indexes and abstracts on library reference shelves; now, many CD-ROM databases have been replaced by Internet databases.

Full-Text Databases

As the World Wide Web expands as a publishing medium, so too does the electronic, online publication of full-text journals and reference material. Three models exist:

1. Individual e-journals (electronic journals) both free and fee-based are available online direct from the publishers.
2. Aggregators negotiate with publishers to distribute their journals, encyclopedias, and directories, managing issues such as licensing, copyright, and subscription costs. Examples of electronic full-text aggregators are Academic Press (IDEAL), ProQuest,

Emerald, JSTOR, EBSCOHost, Gale Databases, xrefer, and Project MUSE.
3. Commercial search vendors provide citation databases with links to full texts, for example, Dialog Information Services (multiple subject areas), LexisNexis (law, news, and business), Ovid (medical journals), and Factiva (business and news).

Citation Databases and the OPAC

How does a citation database differ from a library catalog database?

Library OPACs include records for whole publications such as journals, newspapers, conference proceedings, or books. However, a catalog bibliographic record does not list the individual articles or chapters in the publications it represents. The exception to this is bibliographic records that contain Table of Contents information.

Citation, indexing, and abstracting databases are finding aids to the contents of serial publications with multiple works by different authors. A typical citation record includes the following fields:

- title of article
- author
- title of source publication, with date, volume, and page number details
- subject headings
- abstract (optional)
- links to the full text at another location (optional)

Online bibliographic records and citation database records have a similar structure. Both provide information that enables users to identify and locate the item represented in the record. However, some differences exist. Bibliographic records use the MARC format, but a standard format for displaying information in citation databases does not exist. Data fields are similar across citation databases, but the formats vary and database services use different sets of subject headings or descriptors. Figure 10.1 shows a bibliographic catalog record for an electronic version of *Library Journal,* displaying descriptive, access, and holdings information. The hypertext link Connect to

Title	**Library journal [electronic resource] viaExpanded Academic**

Connect to
Connect to Expanded Academic

Note	Available via the Internet
Uts note	Available to UTS staff and students only
Journal title	Library journal
Other title	Expanded Academic
Lib has	Jan. 1997 +
ISBN OR ISSN	0363-0277

FIGURE 10.1. Bibliographic record for an electronic journal in an OPAC.

Expanded Academic leads library patrons to the online full-text journal supplied by the aggregator Expanded Academic.

In comparison, Figure 10.2 shows a record from an online citation database for an individual article published in *Library Journal*. It includes citation details plus links to the full text of the article in text HTML and PDF formats. The full-text view includes options to e-mail and print the article.

Although separate resources, online catalogs and citations and full-text services are brought together by linking options such as OpenURL and metasearching. See the section on Searching Multiple Online Resources in this chapter for more about these services.

SEARCHING ONLINE DATABASES

Online citation databases use text retrieval systems that divide a database into files of citation records, and alphabetic indexes of words from the records. Search options within field indexes include author, title, subject, abstract, as well as keyword searches across all indexes. Common words, called stop words, are excluded from

> ☐ **It's opening day for METS.** (Digital Libraries)(Metadata Encoding and Transmission
> Mark Standard) Roy Tennant.
> *Library Journal* May 15, 2004 v129 i9 p28(1) (845 words)
> Text | 1 full page PDF |

FIGURE 10.2. Article citation from an online database showing link to full text article.

searches so that the search retrieval is more precise. In a full-text search the context and relationship between words is harder to control and the results may be less precise or relevant.

Retrieval, relevance, and precision are the key elements of database searching. A good database search engine successfully balances these elements to produce results with high relevance and precision but low retrieval. In other words, a small number of citation results that are relevant to the search topic.

Figure 10.3 shows a Basic Search window for an EBSCOHost research database. The default opening search mode is keyword. Options to refine the search are:

- *limit* results to types of publications, specific titles, dates or volumes, peer-reviewed journals, full text, articles with images; and
- *expand* to search the full text of the publication, include all search items, search for related words.

Other search options are within Subjects (subject headings), Publications, Indexes, and Image types (using buttons at top of screen). The Advanced Search offers options to refine a search by selecting a publication type, adding specific citation details, and a Search history of previous searches.

Boolean search operators AND, OR, NOT specify how to combine search words within a record. Proximity operators specify the closeness of words to one another. See Online Searching Skills in Chapter 11 for more on Boolean and proximity operators.

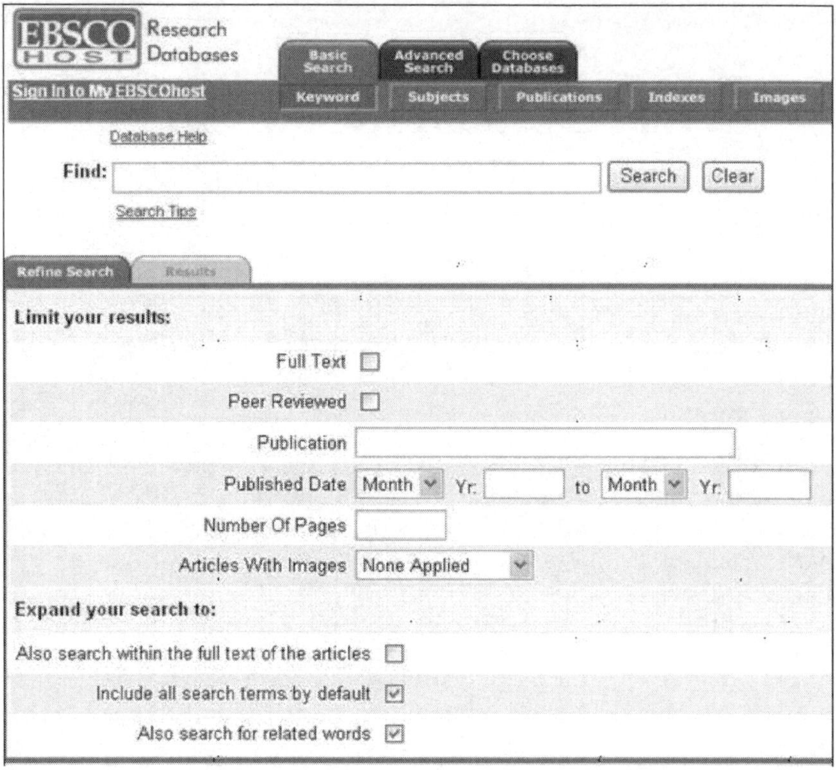

FIGURE 10.3. EBSCOHost citation and full-text database search window showing limit options. Reprinted with permission.

Subject Headings

Most databases discussed in this chapter consist of records created by humans. Publications represented in database records are analyzed and assigned subject headings from an established thesaurus or controlled vocabulary. Records with the same subject headings are grouped together so that a database search on that subject heading retrieves all records.

For example, the topic "Searching multiple databases simultaneously" is described by terms *metasearching, federated searching, universal searching, one search, broadcast search,* and *cross-database searching.*

To retrieve articles on this topic, a keyword search would need to include all these variations. However, if all articles are assigned the subject heading metasearching representing variations of the term, a search on *metasearching* will find all records indexed under that heading.

Keyword searching of title, abstract, and full text can supplement a controlled subject search by finding terms that may not be included in a thesaurus. Starting with a keyword search is sometimes a good way to find appropriate subject headings for a subsequent search.

SEARCHING THE WORLD WIDE WEB

The Web is unstructured whereas records in an online citation database or library catalog are analyzed, described, and indexed. For these reasons finding information in the Web is often more difficult.

The primary tools for searching the Web are search engines. Search engines send out programmed agents known as *robots* or *spiders* to visit millions of Web sites and harvest words. The robots return to the search engine program and deposit their words in a database where they are indexed. It is an automatic process, the only human input being the development of the search engine software and its harvesting mechanisms. There is no analysis of content or use of subject headings, and few structured fields to search within. Web searchers submit search words to search engine interfaces that return lists of Web sites containing those words. Searchers then have to sift through the results to find those that are useful and relevant.

In response to the lack of subject descriptions and standardization in Web sites, the Dublin Core Metadata Initiative (DCMI) <http://dublincore.org> was developed, a fifteen-element set designed to describe the resource content (title, subject, description, language, source, coverage), intellectual property (author, creator, publisher, rights), size, file format, date, type, and identifier (URL, ISBN) of a Web page.

Many Web creators add Dublin Core (DC) metadata elements to the HTML to better describe their Web sites and enhance their retrieval by search engines.

Advanced Searching

In most search engines, the opening search screen presents the simplest search form—just enter your keywords. Many search engines also provide links to advanced searching options to combine words, specify format, language, date updated, and fields where search words should occur. Figure 10.4 shows Google's advanced search screen.

Metasearch Engines

Web metasearch engines or metacrawlers query several separate search engines simultaneously and deliver their results onto one page. Metacrawlers provide greater coverage and retrieval by combining the results. Some metasearch engines are DogPile, Mamma, and Vivisimo. Because all search engines have different techniques or algorithms for collecting words their results vary.

Search engine software and techniques change constantly to improve the gathering of data from the expanding World Wide Web. Keep up to date with developments by visiting Search Engine Watch <http://searchenginewatch.com>.

Evaluating Information

The Web is a diverse information resource that provides access to large amounts of uncontrolled content. Data published on the Web

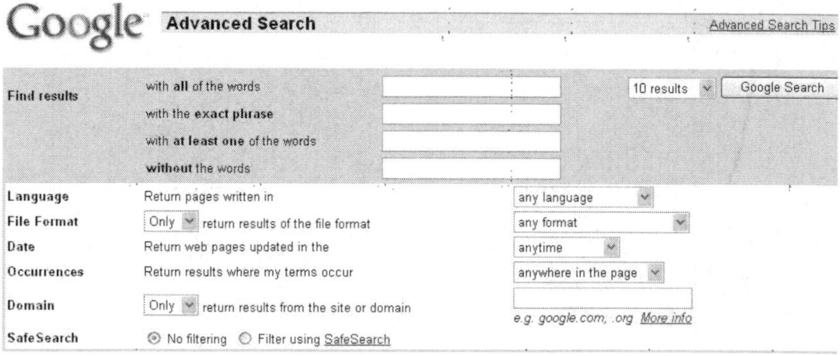

FIGURE 10.4. Google's Advance search screen showing search and limit options. Reprinted with permission.

may be informative, an opinion, unsubstantiated research, home remedies, or political dogma. Web sites are not subject to the editorial control applied to published books and peer-reviewed journals. When using Web sites, or advising library patrons about Web resources, identify the sources, and, if possible, verify information by cross-checking it against other resources. Useful sites for tips on evaluating information are Ten Cs for Evaluating Internet Sources <http://www.uwec.edu/library/Guides/tencs.html>, and Evaluating Internet Information <http://www.library.jhu.edu/elp/useit/evaluate/>.

SEARCHING MULTIPLE ONLINE RESOURCES

As more information has been published on the Web, libraries and information centers have followed this trend by offering multiple services from their Web sites—such as citation and full-text databases, Web search engines, and other library catalogs. The choice may be bewildering for patrons. To simplify the searching experience, libraries can use software and techniques to link citation and full-text databases, and offer cross-database searching.

OpenURL Linking

As discussed in Chapter 7, OpenURL linking is a NISO standard that allows libraries to create links between catalogs and databases, enabling a search strategy or citation to be carried to other resources. The linking can be context sensitive, so that some links are offered only if certain conditions apply. Libraries customize the resources that appear in the link screens.

Figure 10.5 shows an example of the OpenURL linking software called WebBridge. An OPAC record shows a book titled *Java Database Best Practices.* Selecting the WebBridge button opens a second window with options to search beyond the OPAC:

- a magazine or journal article using a subject heading from the bibliographic record, Java (computer program language)
- another library catalog, SFU, searching for the subject heading
- Amazon.com, for the title *Java Database Best Practices*
- a Web search engine Google for Java (computer program language)

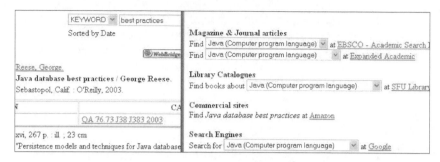

FIGURE 10.5. An OPAC search result (left) with WebBridge button offering OpenURL linking to more resource options on the right.

Federated or Metasearching

In Chapter 8 we discussed federated or metasearching, a technique that searches multiple databases simultaneously. This technology enables the grouping of databases by subject clusters, formats of material, or alphabetically. A metasearch carries one search strategy across both bibliographic and full-text databases that do not share a common thesaurus or index. Instead of searching many times, patrons do not have to repeat the search and need to use only one search interface.

Access and Licensing

Electronic full texts are offered by many libraries and information centers. Links from an online database citation or OPAC, provide the full text of articles online for local downloading or printing.

Online citation and full-text databases are licensed to libraries under two different models. The first licenses the database services on a subscription basis, whereby libraries pay an annual subscription fee to provide unlimited access to their patrons. No costs are passed on to the patrons when they conduct database searches from within a library or center or remotely.

The second method charges a usage fee either at a flat rate or per-minute rate for connect time, sometimes with a fee for obtaining full texts. Libraries using these services generally conduct database searches on behalf of their clients to minimize costs instead of offering end-user searching.

Libraries negotiate licensing, access, and subscription plans with database vendors. Access to database services from within a library or institutional space is authenticated by the IP or Internet address range of the installed computers. To enable remote access, libraries must identify the users as library patrons. When a patron selects an option to connect to the online database from the library's Web OPAC (for example, the link Connect to Expanded Academic in Figure 10.1), the authentication software verifies that the patron is registered with the library, and completes the connection to the online database. If a patron is not verified, access is denied.

Harvesting Digital Resources

For several decades the distribution of preprints of scholarly journal articles in advance of their official publication has been common within scientific, research, and academic communities. In the 1990s, preprints were converted to electronic formats, called e-prints, and stored in archives or repositories on the Internet. Authors contribute their papers to the archives, enabling scientists and researchers around the world to read them online before they are published in journals. arXiv was the first e-print service, and was developed by Paul Ginsparg at the Los Alamos National Laboratories. The arXiv e-print service covers the fields of physics, mathematics, nonlinear science, computer science, and quantitative biology <http://arxiv.org/>.

E-print technology has been adopted by other scientific communities. Some examples are PubMed Central, the U.S. National Library of Medicine's unrestricted digital archive of life sciences journals <http://www.pubmedcentral.nih.gov/>, and the Public Library of Science's medical journals online <http://www.publiclibraryofscience.org/>.

The Open Archives Initiative Metadata Harvesting Protocol (OAI-MHP) enables the searching of multiple archives and collections of e-prints. External programs similar to Web search engines harvest record metadata from multiple servers and store the details in a central searchable database. The metadata include a URL that points back to the database records they describe.

The metadata harvesting protocol has expanded beyond e-print archives. As an open protocol it can be used by any World Wide Web-based database, library online catalogs, repository of electronic journal papers, or other digital objects, both nonprofit and commercial. An excellent example of Open Archives Metadata Harvesting Protocol is OAIster <http://www.oaister.org> from the University of Michigan. This is a searchable database of public digital resources from hundreds of academic and research institutions worldwide who wish to share their data. OAIster provides access to scholarly information from the "hidden Web"—information in Internet-accessible databases, including library catalogs that are not accessible to Web search engines. Figure 10.6 shows the OAIster search interface with options to limit by field and resource type, and a definition of a digital resource. PictureAustralia <http://www.pictureaustralia.org> is a database of digital images covering all aspects of Australian life that are harvested from multiple online sources in Australia and elsewhere using the Open Archives Metadata Harvesting Protocol.

Searching for information in the age of the Internet occurs in a rapidly changing environment. Libraries and information centers face the challenge of bringing these services to patrons and organizing them into easy-to-use interfaces.

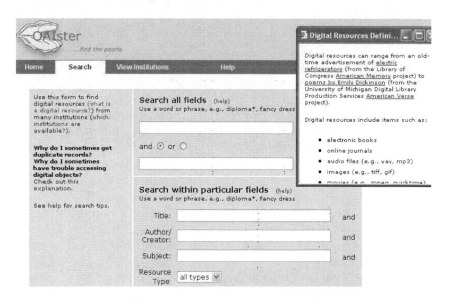

FIGURE 10.6. University of Michigan's OAIster metadata harvester search interface and pop-up window showing definition of its digital resources. Reprinted with permission.

REVIEW QUESTIONS

1. Define a citation and a full-text database.
2. What are the differences between structured database and Web searching?
3. Explain the difference between a Web metasearch engine and the process of meta- or federated searching.
4. Explain what the metadata harvesting protocol is used for.

Chapter 11

Computer Skills and Competencies

TERMINOLOGY

Boolean operators: Connect words used to combine search terms in database searching.

CSS (cascading style sheets): Files that define styles in HTML files for the World Wide Web.

DTD (document type definition): Defines the attributes of elements in an XML file.

function keys: Computer keys programmed for specific software functions.

 HTML (hypertext markup language): Specifies the display of documents on the World Wide Web.

information retrieval: Search for information stored in online databases.

keyboard shortcuts: Key combinations that provide shortcuts to software functions.

proximity operators: Connecting words that determine the closeness of terms to one another in a database search.

style sheets: Files that define style elements for HTML (CSS) and XML (XSLT) documents.

XHTML (extensible hypertext markup language): HTML reformulated in XML; the successor to HTML.

XML (extensible markup language): A universal format to describe documents for digital publication.

XSL (extensible style sheet): A language that transforms XML documents into HTML to display on the World Wide Web.

XSLT (extensible style language transformation): An XML based language used in XSL style sheets to transform XML documents into other formats such as HTML.

This chapter looks at three skill areas relevant to computers in libraries and information centers: using computers, online searching, and creating content for the World Wide Web.

COMPUTER SKILLS

Computers are an essential part of work in library and information centers, as in many workplaces. Libraries use both IBM-compatible (PCs) and Apple Macintosh personal computers (MACs). The two have similar file management structure and keyboard, with a few differences. The first part of this chapter includes some shortcuts and tips to supplement basic computer skills.

The Keyboard

To use a computer, super-fast typing speeds are not essential, but being familiar with the keyboard and its options is an advantage. Computer keyboards use the QWERTY layout that was developed for manual typewriters. QWERTY stands for the first six letters in the top alphabet row of a keyboard. The layout was designed to prevent individual typewriter keys from sticking together if used in rapid succession, by ensuring that the most common keys were not selected at the same time. QWERTY is not the most natural keyboard arrangement, but typists and computer users have used it for many years. Computer keyboards do not have the arms or levers for keys that are used in typewriters, and thus do not need to separate keys, but the QWERTY layout is still popular in computer keyboards. Dvorak is an alternative keyboard format for computers that places vowels and common consonants closer together and easier to reach. Few keyboards are constructed using the Dvorak scheme, but a QWERTY computer keyboard can be reprogrammed for Dvorak through software conversion programs.

Keyboard Shortcuts

Function keys are the keys numbered F1 to F12 at the top of a keyboard. Keyboard combinations for frequently used activities are programmed into function keys. For example, within library system modules, function keys defined for different modes enable quicker movement between modes.

Keyboard shortcuts are combinations of keys that are alternatives to the mouse, used to reduce the number of keystrokes, i.e., times a key is touched. In a busy library environment when keying data, fewer keystrokes speeds up the process. Universal keyboard shortcuts are part of many software programs, including library systems. For example, shortcuts for editing data are activated by pressing the CTRL key in combination with a letter key:

CTRL C = copy
CTRL X = cut
CTRL V = paste

Other shortcuts provide quick access to drop-down menus such as File or Edit. The ALT key pressed with an underlined menu letter opens a drop-down menu. Selecting another underlined letter opens a menu function. For example, in Figure 11.1, ALT E opens the Edit menu, and the letter F opens the Find window, which enables searching within a document. Or press the CTRL and F keys in succession to open the Find window.

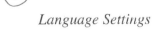

Tip: Always save, save, save as you work! Use the keyboard shortcut CTRL S for fast saves!

Language Settings

Library and information centers may have diverse user populations and staff who read and speak different languages. Online catalogs

FIGURE 11.1 Edit menu on a PC Windows application activated by pressing the
ALT E keys.

may have bibliographic records for multilingual or international material that include language diacritics. Computer operating systems
have Language or Regional settings with language input options that
remap the keyboard to incorporate different symbols, or convert keyboard input from one language to other language scripts. Such settings enable input of different languages.

The Mouse

With most software the mouse supplements the keyboard for
screen navigation. The mouse plugs into the computer and uses infra-
red technology to interact remotely with the computer, or a touchpad
built into the keyboard. PCs have two mouse buttons, left and right,
and each button has default settings. For example, on a right mouse

the left button points to data on the screen, and the right button opens hidden shortcut menus. A Macintosh mouse does not have separate buttons; instead press the left or right side of the mouse to activate the settings. The mouse's left and right button orientation can be swapped through the computer's Control Panel. Figure 11.2 shows mouse button settings for a PC. Note the Auto Scroll feature, activated by pressing both buttons.

Tip: The mouse has hidden functions for text editing. Place your mouse pointer on text and triple click to highlight or select a whole record field or paragraph, instead of dragging the mouse across the text. Double click to highlight a word. Hold down the mouse button and drag selected text to drop in another location.

Using Software

Computer skills are transferable across different programs. Almost every piece of software—library systems, e-mail, telnet programs, Web

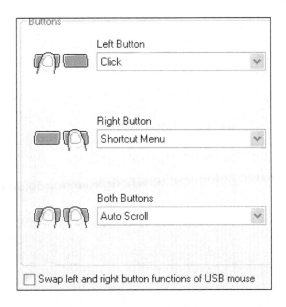

FIGURE 11.2. Mouse button control panel in a Windows operating system.

browsers, and Java applications—are designed with the same drop-down menu structure shown in Figure 11.1.

Explore the computer settings and features, but before making any changes, note the original settings in case they need to be restored. Integrated library system software settings such as color and font size may be separate from those of the personal computer's operating system. When multiple users share logins, access to system settings may be disabled to prevent changes. The library system administrator may be able to adjust settings individually for those who have special visual or display needs.

ONLINE SEARCHING SKILLS

The skills used in searching online databases, often referred to as information retrieval skills, are applicable in most searching environments—online catalogs, citation and full-text databases, and Web search engines.

Search Techniques

In an online search, the more accurately the topic is described the better the retrieval. To achieve this, search techniques specify how words relate to each other in the same context.

Boolean Operators

Boolean operators are logical operators that combine terms and concepts in a search strategy. The operators are:

> AND—narrows a search result by looking for records where all specified terms exist
> OR—widens a search by combining alternative search terms or synonyms
> NOT—excludes records that contain specified terms; also expressed as AND NOT

Boolean operators are represented visually by Venn diagrams as shown in Figure11.3.

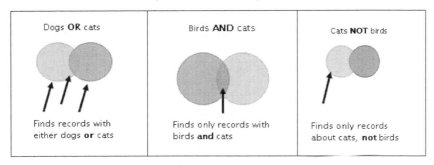

FIGURE 11.3. Boolean operators OR, AND, NOT.

Parentheses combine more than one Boolean operator within a search statement to specify the order in which to apply the operators. This is known as nested searching.

For example, to find material about the behavior of birds with either cats or dogs use the following nested strategy:

(dogs OR cats) AND birds

This strategy searches for records that contain the words *dogs* or *cats,* and within those records, retrieves only records that also contain the word *birds.*

Proximity Operators

Proximity operators determine the closeness of terms to one another. The Boolean operator AND searches for terms occur only in the same sentence, field (e.g., title, abstract), or paragraph, but may not be related or in the same context. Proximity operators specify a closer relationship between words. The most common proximity operators are:

- *adjacent* or *adj* requires that terms appear next to each other. For example, *round adj robin* may retrieve the phrase *round robin,* or *robin round.* Web search engines use double quotations to express phrases, e.g., "round robin"
- *near* specifies a number of terms (the number is set by the search service) that can appear between the search terms, e.g., *round*

> ***near** robin,* may retrieve the phrases *round robin,* or *round birds like a robin,* or a *robin has round eyes*
> - *within* specifies a number of terms to appear between search terms, e.g., *round **within2** robin* retrieves *round* and *robin* with up to two terms between them

If no operator appears with multiple keywords the search system applies one of the following operators by default:

- *Adjacent,* where words appear next to each other (most narrow)
- Boolean AND, where *all* words must exist within the same record field
- Boolean OR, where *any* word can exist within a record (broadest)

If a search is unsuccessful, a search service may apply more default operators. The first may be *adjacency,* words as a phrase; if no results, a system may use Boolean AND, words in the same sentence; if still unsuccessful a search may be broadened to look for any of the words entered (Boolean OR).

Figure 11.4 shows results from an OPAC keyword search for *marine harvesting.* Only the first title, *Harvesting the Ocean,* contains both keywords (shown in the full record) and is relevant. The marks in the left column represent levels of relevance.

OPACs, citation databases, and Web search engines produce different results depending on their default or implied operator setting.

■ ■ ■ ■ ▲	Harvesting the ocean.
	Location: Curriculum Collection (Level 3) *Call Number: GC1016.5 .H3*
■ ■ ■ ▲	Men and machines in sugar cane harvesting / Department of Labour and National Service..
	Title has multiple holdings
■ ■ ■ ▲	Where does food come from ? [picture].
	Location: Curriculum Collection (Level 3) *Call Number: TX355 .F656/no*
■ ■ ■ ▲	Studies of a light harvesting chlorophyll-a protein complex [manuscript] / by Francis Peter Sharples.

FIGURE 11.4. Result of a keyword search on marine harvesting in an OPAC.

Most systems allow you to override the default by inserting another operator into a keyword search.

Truncation

Truncation, or wildcarding, is the use of a designated symbol such as $, *, #,? to search for variations in the spelling or case (singular or plural) of search terms.

Two truncation options are:

- *single letter* or embedded truncation, to search variant spellings within a word, e.g., *wom?n* to find *women* or *woman.* The embedded truncation symbol may also represent no letter, so that *colo?r* will find *color* as well as *colour.*
- *multiple letter* truncation, placed at the end of a word or part of a word to find plurals or words derived from the same stem. Placement of the truncation symbol affects retrieval, e.g., *libr** finds *library, libraries, librarian, librarianship,* but also *libra, libran, libretto, librettist.*

Searching Indexed Fields

Online catalogs and subject-based citation databases store data in separate indexes such as subject headings, author names, and titles. Select a specific index to search within, and only records containing the search terms in the specified field are retrieved. For example, a search for a name in the author index in an OPAC retrieves all works by that author. In online catalogs this is called phrase searching because the system looks for the entire author name or phrase, searching from left to right. To find out more about phrase searching see Chapter 8.

Keyword searching differs from phrase searching in these ways:

- A keyword index includes words from many fields, e.g., title, author, subject, abstract, contents. A general keyword search finds terms located anywhere in a document.
- Keyword index searches in specific fields, e.g., a title, subject, or author keyword, find words in any order, not left to right as with phrase searching.

Combining Search Statements

Some databases can combine multiple search statements with Boolean operators. For example, to find documents about the use of Boolean operators in either Internet or online searching use this strategy:

> *Internet searching*
> OR *online searching*
> AND *(Boolean ADJ operators)*

Figure 11.5 shows this search strategy in a Web OPAC advanced keyword search form.

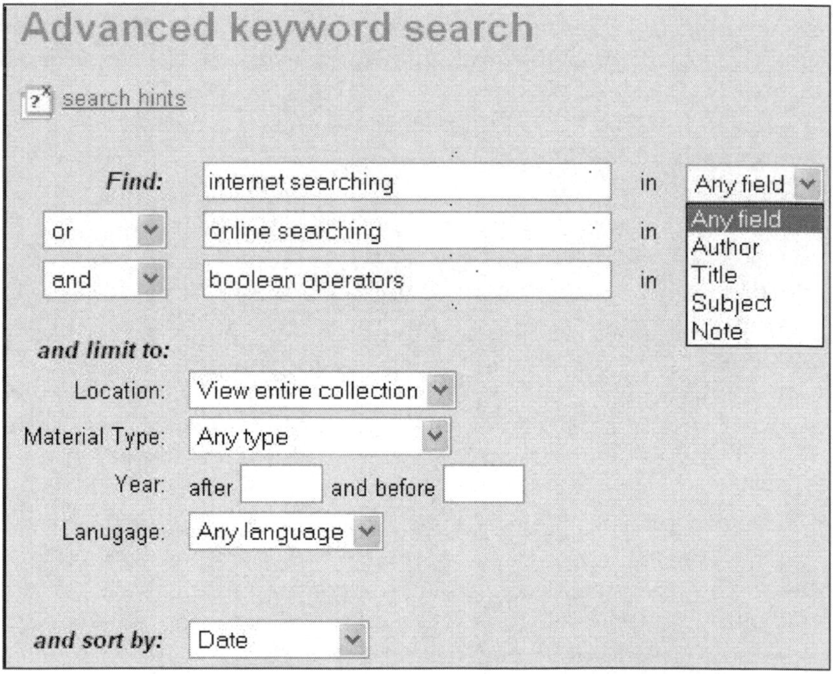

FIGURE 11.5. Combined search statements in an OPAC advanced keyword search.

Web Searching Skills

Search engines find material published on the World Wide Web. Their search techniques are more simplified than those used with database searching, but most search engines offer advanced features that can make a difference to your search results.

In any search engine, the more specific the search terms are, the more successful a search. Enter as many terms as necessary to describe the search concepts. Most search engines try to match ALL of the terms, by default. Some search engines offer logical operators and express them using symbols:

- + requires terms to be present (Boolean AND)
- – excludes terms from a search (Boolean NOT)
- double quotation marks for phrase *(proximity)* searching.

For example *"database searching"—Internet* finds Web pages that discuss database searching, but not on the Internet.

Field searching is offered by search engines, although it is more limited than with structured databases, such as online catalogs, because Web pages do not have many separate fields. Fields such as title, URL, link, and site or host, are searched using advanced search options.

For example, the search Google:*metadata searching* looks for Web pages in which the words *metadata searching* appear anywhere in the page. The search in the title using *allintitle:metadata searching* is more precise, returning only Web pages where the words appear in the title. This result set is smaller and the pages are more relevant because words in the title are more indicative of the subject.

Note that advanced search options vary among search engines. To find out which options are offered check a search engine's Help or Search Tips pages.

Relevance Ranking

Because of the millions of documents on the Web, search engines rank or sort results so that the most relevant Web pages appear at the top of a results list. The ranking is based on built-in algorithms such as where search terms appear (e.g., title, first paragraph), and how many times they appear. Internet searchers are unaware of the ranking algorithms, and most search engines do not advertise their methods. Some commercial search engines accept payment from Web developers in return for providing higher rankings for their Web sites.

The Google search engine <http://www.google.com> uses a ranking principle based on popularity. This method ranks a Web site according to the number of sites linking to it, an indication of the site's popularity: the more links a site has the higher is its ranking. Often it turns out that the most popular sites are useful, and this procedure has made Google highly successful. The hunt for the most efficient search methods is an ongoing challenge for search engines and developers.

Preparing a Search

Before going live with an online search it helps to plan and write down the extent and parameters of a search. Following are some suggested steps. Note that not all these options are offered by every search service.

1. *Format.* Think about the type of material needed as this may determine which resources to search. For example, books, journal articles, and Web sites, or formats such as images, software files, films, music or audio.
2. *Concepts.* Define search concepts or elements, for example, a specific work by a named author, a subject, or geographic location.
3. *Terms.* Select the terms for the concepts. For an author search, should the name be truncated to search for variant spellings? Does an authorized heading (name or subject) exist?
4. *Operators.* How should the search terms combine? Which Boolean or proximity operators should you use? Can all search terms be in one statement or should separate statements be used?
5. *Fields.* Specify fields to search within, e.g., author, subject, title, or keyword. Note the difference between a keyword search across multiple fields, and a subject search within the index of controlled subject headings (see Chapter 8).
6. *Time.* Determine the time frame or date range if necessary, e.g., published in the current year only, or limited to a range of years.
7. *Review, refine, and revise.* View the search results and modify the search strategy to add more terms, or remove terms from a

search. Search on a subject heading or descriptor from a relevant record to expand or narrow the results. If retrieved items are not relevant, or not sufficient in number, try keyword searching or search the full text, if available. Sometimes a search term is not used in a title, abstract, or subject heading list, but may appear in the full text.

8. *Expand your horizons.* A search may begin in a library OPAC, and then extend to a citation or full-text database for journal publications (OpenURL linking). Or search a number of resources at once, grouped by subject or format, using meta- or federated search services.

CREATING CONTENT FOR THE WORLD WIDE WEB

Chapter 8 looked at the use of HTML to create and customize library Web OPACs. HTML editing software programs have made HTML creation almost as easy as word processing. However, some knowledge of the structure of HTML helps to understand how it works.

HTML consists of *tags* enclosed in angle brackets and *attributes* that define different elements and design features of an HTML document. Some tags and their functions are shown in Table 11.1.

Figure 11.6 shows a segment of an HTML file. The coding within the angle brackets does not display in the Web browser, only the text between the angle brackets and any image files. For example, the hypertext link <A href="mainpage.html">Return to Main Page</A> displays the words Return to Main Page as a hypertext link on the Web site. The tag <IMG src="roses.jpg"> is an instruction to display the image file roses.jpg. Figure 11.7 shows the HTML file in Figure 11.6 from a Web browser.

HTML files and image files are stored on a Web server connected to the Internet. Web browsers display the data and files according to the HTML coding.

An HTML file is created as plain text and saved with a file name and extension of .html or .htm, for example, roses.html. A single Web site includes multiple HTML files linked together. CSS (cascading style sheets) enhance and control style formatting of Web pages, such as fonts, margins, line spacing, borders, and colors.

TABLE 11.1. HTML tags.

Tag	Function
<html> </html>	Opening and closing tags
<head> </head>	Contains data that do not display in a Web browser, e.g., title metatags
<title> </title>	Web page title that displays in the title bar
<body> </body>	Defines color and link settings. Includes the attributes:
<body bg color=>	Background color
<body text=>	Body text
<body link=>	Color of hypertext links
<body vlink=>	Color of followed links
<body alink=>	Color of links when clicked
<h?> </h?>	Specifies size of headers, from 1 (largest)-6 (smallest)
<b></b>	Denotes bold text
<i></i>	Denotes italic text
<font size =?></font>	Font size
<font color=?></font>	Font color
<a href="URL"></a>	Creates a hypertext link
<a name="NAME"></a>	Creates a target within a document
<a href="#NAME"></a>	Creates a link to a target in a document
<p></p>	Inserts a new paragraph
 	Inserts a line break
<ol></ol>	Creates a numbered (ordered) list
<ul></ul>	Creates a bulleted or unnumbered list
<li></li>	Denotes an entry in a list, adding a number or bullet
<img src="filename">	Inserts an image file, with attributes such as:
<img src="name" align=?>	Aligns an image
<img src="name" border=?>	Places a border around an image

```
<HTML>
<HEAD>
<TITLE>Name of page</TITLE>
<META http-equiv=Content-Type content="text/html; charset=windows-1252">
</HEAD>
<BODY>
A beautiful bride with roses in her hair.
<p>
<IMG src="roses.jpg">
<p>
<A href="mainpage.html">Return to Main Page</A>
<p>
</BODY>
</HTML>
```

FIGURE 11.6. An example of an HTML coded file.

FIGURE 11.7. The HTML file from Figure 11.6 seen through a Web browser. Reprinted with permission by Richard Booker.

HTML is changing as the Web and the Internet develop. It is an open public standard maintained and developed by the World Wide Web Consortium, a nonprofit organization <http://www.w3.org/>. To learn more about HTML, consult the many available books, Web sites, and HTML editing software.

Understanding XML

④ XML (extensible markup language), is a standard developed by the World Wide Web Consortium to describe the structure of digital objects and documents for publishing on the Web. It is a free, widely adopted, cross-platform software and hardware independent format that enables the exchange and reuse of data. XML extends and enhances HTML; both are derived from SGML, the standard generalized markup language used in publishing.

XML is an open and flexible standard that is easy to define and customize in a markup structure, unlike HTML, which strictly follows the HTML tag structure and rules. XML uses the syntax of starting and ending tags to mark up information elements, for example <journal></journal> may indicate a journal record. Tag elements follow these guidelines:

- main elements (parent)
- child elements (subelements)
- attributes modify elements and subelements, e.g., <name ="personal">
- a wrapper tag may bind together child elements, but contain no data, e.g.,

```
<titleinfo>                           ← wrapper tag
<title>Learning XML:</title>          ←
<subtitle>an introduction</subtitle>  ← subelements
<chapter>Chapter 1</chapter>          ←
</titleinfo>                          ← wrapper tag
```

The following rules apply when creating XML files:

- Files must begin with an XML statement such as <?xml version="1.0"?>
- Tags must always be closed with a slash <title>...</title>

- Tags are case sensitive and if capitalization is used it must be in both opening and closing tags
- A root element marks the beginning and end of a file, e.g., <book> </book>
- Element names can contain letters, numbers, and other characters
- Element names must not start with a number or punctuation
- Element names must not start with the letters xml (or XML or Xml)
- Element names cannot contain spaces

XML describes only the structure of documents. An XSL style sheet or HTML CSS (cascading style sheet) created separately and referenced within the XML file specifies the formatting of colors and fonts for display on the Web.

Each XML file uses a DTD (Document Type Definition) to define the building blocks, elements, attributes, and how XML tags should relate to one another. A DTD is referenced in the XML document, or externally in an XML schema. DTDs are available freely for adaptation to suit the XML material and user community and companies develop private DTDs for proprietary XML products. The XML example shown in Figure 11.8 includes references to DTD and XSL files.

XML has many applications that are used in libraries and information centers for developing databases, procedures, and as a flexible format for different record types. Some examples are archival finding, and the harvesting of records from one database to another (Tennant,

```
<?xml version="1.0"?>
<!DOCTYPE HTML PUBLIC "-//W3C//DTD HTML 4.01 Transitional//EN"
"http://www.w3.org/TR/html4/loose.dtd">
<?xml-stylesheet href="test.xsl" type="text/xsl"?>
<presentation>
<titleinfo>
<title>Learning XML: </title>
<subtitle>an instructional guide</subtitle>
</titleinfo>
<chapter>Introduction to XML</chapter>
<section> What is XML?</section>
<section> How does XML work?</section>
</presentation>
```

FIGURE 11.8. A sample XML file.

2002). You can create XML files manually or with an XML editor program. Many Web sites and books provide more information on XML.

XHTML (extensible hypertext markup language) is the World Wide Web Consortium standard that extends HTML as an XML application to create richer Web pages and other devices such as cell phones, wireless communicators, and computer desktops.

REVIEW QUESTIONS

1. What is the purpose of function keys on a computer keyboard?
2. What is the keyboard shortcut for saving a document?
3. What is the function of Boolean and proximity operators in online database searching?
4. Describe the difference between XML and HTML.

Chapter 12

Future Directions

Predicting the future of technology is like writing horoscopes: guesses and estimates are based on typical and possible characteristics, or from looking at past and current behavior. The Internet is an open vehicle for a multitude of ideas, making the future unpredictable and exciting. This final chapter looks at trends in computers affecting the library and information world.

PERSONAL COMPUTERS

The use of personal computers to access information in library catalogs, databases, and the Internet will continue, but computers will get smaller. Monitors or display units have become flatter and smaller. Other computer hardware is likely to shrink in size also, becoming more compact and modular so that separate parts are removable, replaceable, and exchangeable.

Personal digital assistants (PDAs) take on more functions of the personal computer such as e-mail and Web browsing, combined with voice and text messaging. Searching the library catalog via the Web from your cell phone or PDA is widely available.

NETWORKING AND THE INTERNET

Networking capabilities and access will be more flexible, with the expansion of wireless network technology. As more people access information online, remotely (from outside a library building), as well as from within, the nature and function of the library building will change. It will no longer be the primary place to locate information, but a place to meet, gather, study, and socialize. More virtual and digital libraries will offer vast amounts of information online. The Internet will continue to transform the library and information world in many ways. Privacy and security of online personal data will continue to be a challenging task for libraries.

XML (extensible markup language) will be the primary format for describing the structure of digital objects and documents, with XHTML, an XML version of HTML, already replacing HTML as the markup language for the Web.

DIGITAL LIBRARIES AND ELECTRONIC PUBLISHING

Digitizing of data and electronic publishing for information provision and preservation will continue to be a priority for organizations, companies, businesses, and governments. The printed book will not disappear as a format, but refinements in the e-book medium will extend its usage allowing online previews and updates. How much will the widespread use of the Web as a publishing medium replace the print format material collected by libraries? Will the incorporation of digital libraries with the traditional or physical library collection be accomplished seamlessly? Will libraries continue to select and collect digital as well as print material, or will other agencies overtake libraries in the management of digital collections? Users search online rather than use print materials and expect their needs to be fully met with digital, online material. As budgets are challenged by the costs of print publications, libraries will search for different models for collecting materials. Shared acquisition and resources among libraries, with access to one another's collections is one option. Libraries may work with publishers to acquire monographs electronically and the digital rights to reproduce and distribute the material.

Libraries and information centers license access to digital material such as full-text electronic journal databases, but have no control over preserving and managing the existence of such materials. If an electronic journal subscription is canceled, the library no longer retains access to the previous digital volumes. Strategies must be developed to assist in the long-term preservation and archiving of digital materials, and of print monographs for digital distribution.

In the future we will see the growth of the Internet as a viable and accessible publishing medium. Online catalogs incorporate Weblogs (blogs), online newspapers, RSS (Rich Site Summary) feeds with e-journals, e-books, and whatever comes next.

INTEGRATED LIBRARY MANAGEMENT SYSTEMS

Library systems have been the foundation of automation in libraries and information centers since the 1970s. In-house systems gave way to proprietary systems in the 1990s, with turnkey models bundling together hardware and software. One trend is the unbundling of software, and the selling of separate pieces. Libraries integrate different software into their systems, combining modules and products. As software becomes more interoperable (able to interact with other platforms and products) the integration of parts will be easier.

The option of purchasing open-source software developed and adapted by organizations and communities, and not tied to a proprietary program, will continue. Locally managed and supported systems will use a mixture of open-source and proprietary software, similar to earlier in-house library system models. Figure 12.1 shows the changes in library system software.

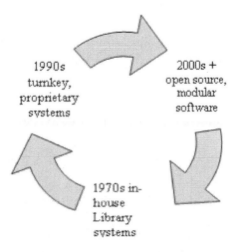

FIGURE 12.1. Developments in integrated library system software.

BIBLIOGRAPHIC STANDARDS
AND PRACTICES

MARC, the cataloging format standard, has limitations for describing digital data. The development of extended metadata schemes for describing documents, starting the Dublin Core Metadata Initiative, has moved beyond MARC. In the future, MARC, and AACR2, the standards for describing catalog records, will be extended, surpassed, and incorporated with other standards and formats. New standards, software tools, and systems will emerge to store, output, search, and display metadata from a variety of bibliographic or related standards. Existing bibliographic standards will work with related interoperable and platform-independent standards such as the Open Archives Initiative-Protocol for Metadata Harvesting (OAI-PMH) and the Simple Object Access Protocol (SOAP).

The use of XML as a format for bibliographic records is growing, enabling the exchange of records between a range of resources or repositories to add to local online catalogs. For example, OCLC, the bibliographic utility, has restructured WorldCat, its bibliographic database, into an XML-structured database that accepts records in any format.

FRBR, the Functional Requirements for Bibliographic Records, is a recommendation of the International Federation of Library Associations (IFLA) to restructure catalog databases to reflect the conceptual structure of information resources. FRBR transforms cataloging practices, focusing on cataloging more than the physical piece in a bibliographic record. It brings together the original piece or work and all its artistic expressions, manifestations (versions or editions), and items in the same context. The intention of FRBR is to simplify bibliographic cataloging and search and retrieval, and reduce duplication of search results. With FRBR, when users search the catalog for a title the result includes all details for the title's variations, rather than a list of separate bibliographic records.

In conjunction with its FRBR research, OCLC is developing the xISBN database that groups together all ISBNs for titles in OCLC's WorldCat database, representing all variations and editions of a work.

BEYOND THE OPAC

Library Web sites are the public focal point of a library's online catalog and services. Links to indexing and abstracting databases, electronic books, and journals are incorporated into bibliographic records and linked to from the Web site. Further portal development will provide a smoother, seamless incorporation of electronic data, including OpenURL linking to relevant resources and extended context-sensitive searching.

Studies report that the use of the online public access catalog is declining in academic libraries (Greenstein, 2004). Users are skipping the catalog and physical collections, directly searching online databases and journals, and the Web for other information. The demand for desktop delivery of materials will continue to increase, going beyond the traditional function of an online catalog that leads users to the library's local collection.

Development of personal portal software will allow library users to build their own electronic resources interface, with links to online databases, online catalogs, and selected Web sites. MyLibrary <http://dewey.library.nd.edu/mylibrary/> is an example of this kind of development. Its purpose is to reduce information overload by allowing patrons to select as little or as much information as needed for their personal pages. By using Weblogs (blogs), bibliographic reference management software, and OpenURL link resolvers, individuals can create their own, personal, Web-based resource collection <http://curtis.med.yale.edu/dchud/writings/blm.html>.

ONLINE SEARCHING

Improved structuring of Web pages to provide better search engine results will occur, along with the filtering of Web information to improve research results. Reliance on Web search engines means that researchers and library users are ignoring a large amount of digital and print information. Search engines refine search functions to reach the large proportion of the "deep" or "invisible, hidden" Web, i.e., data stored in databases, online catalogs, and other repositories that are inaccessible to search robots. Web search engines will incorporate structured database information in their sweep of the Web. For example, the OCLC Open WorldCat project adds bibliographic records in the WorldCat database, and to the index of the search engines Yahoo and Google. WorldCat results lead to an OCLC page with options to enter a zip or postal code, state, province or country and find libraries that hold the retrieved item. The Google Book Search project <http://books.google.com> is working with major libraries to digitize books and provide the full text of those out of copyright, and sample for books that are still in copyright.

Federated searching crosses multiple databases using a single search interface. This is leading to the separation of search interfaces from content in structured databases. In turn, the application of structured search interfaces to Web search engines will enhance the searching capabilities of the Web. If search engines can harness the wider Web, libraries may license search engine software to offer one-stop searching of all resources within a library's physical and digital domain.

REFERENCE SERVICES

The use of online virtual reference services (e.g., Ask a Librarian, AskNow) will continue because they use the popular media (online, instant messaging, chat). Access from home, twenty-four-hour availability, sharing the same medium (computer to computer) are some of the reasons for the popularity of online references. Anonymity is another reason: people may be often reluctant to ask questions in person, or in front of others, and find it difficult to formulate a question succinctly. Online references enable more time to prepare, plan, and interact anonymously.

Help or assistance in physical library buildings has separated into Information (where to locate), and Research or Reference Services departments. The trend in the 1990s to rename reference and research departments and desks as Information Services has reversed. Now, the two levels of assistance are separate because they each have a different focus. Information is location based, whereas reference and research assistance has moved out of the physical space into the digital, online arena. Separate reference desks are disappearing, replaced by online and appointment-only services.

SKILLS AND COMPETENCIES

Increased familiarity with computers will speed up processing and encourage software enhancements and development within libraries. As changes occur in the bibliographic structure and standards, library cataloging and other technical services staff will learn new formats and rules (as happened with the incorporation of Dublin Core metadata tagging schemes).

As more users independently conduct their own searches, the provision of search services by library staff will change to instruction and assistance, rather than mediated searching. This trend will continue with online tutorial instruction complementing online searching and face-to-face instruction. Library vendor training offers combinations of online tutorial instruction and immediate or synchronous Web conferencing.

Technology and computing skills will continue to be a major requirement in future library and information workplaces. Embrace them; understand how the programs, systems, and networks link together, and your work will be fulfilling!

Bibliography

Anglo-American cataloguing rules. Second edition, 2002 revision (2002). Chicago: American Library Association.

Australian National University (2004). *Assistive technology in universities.* Available online <http://www.anu.edu.au/disabilities/atproject/index.php>.

Banerjee, Kyle (September 2002). How does XML help libraries? *Computers in libraries,* 22 (8). Available online <http://www.infotoday.com/cilmag/sep02/Banerjee.htm>.

Banerjee, Kyle (2002). Improving interlibrary loan with XML. In Tennant, Roy (Ed.), *XML in libraries* (pp. 31-44). New York, NY: Neal-Schuman Publishers.

Berners-Lee, Tim and Mark Fischetti (2000). *Weaving the Web: The past, present and future of the World Wide Web by its inventor.* New York: HarperCollins Publishers.

Billings, Harold (2002). *Magic and hypersystems: Constructing the information-sharing library.* Chicago: American Library Association.

Bush, Vannevar (1945). As we may think. *The Atlantic Monthly,* July, *176* (1), 101-108.

Cailliau, Robert and James Gillies (2000). *How the Web was born: The story of the World Wide Web.* Oxford: Oxford University Press.

Caplan, Priscilla (2003). *Metadata fundamentals for all librarians.* Chicago: American Library Association.

Castro, Elizabeth (2003). *HTML for the World Wide Web With XHTML and CSS: Visual quickstart guide.* Berkeley, CA: Peachpit Press.

Chen, Li and Joyce White Mills (2002). A primer for today's machines. *Computers in Libraries* (July/August), 15-22.

Cohn, John M., Ann L. Kelsey, and Keith Michael Fiels (2002). *Planning for integrated systems and technologies: A how-to-do-it manual for librarians.* Second United Kingdom edition. London: Facet Publishing.

Council on Library and Information Resources (2004). *Access in the future tense.* Available online <http://www.clir.org/pubs/reports/pub126/contents.html>.

Crane, Tim. (2003). *The mechanical mind: A philosophical introduction to minds, machines and mental representation.* Second edition. London: New York: Routledge and Paul.

Dublin Core Metadata Initiative (DCMI) (2004). Available online <http://dublincore.org/>.

Ferguson, Stuart and Rodney Headl (2003). *Computers for librarians: An introduction to the electronic library.* Third edition. Wagga Wagga, NSW, Australia: Charles Sturt University.

Furrie, Betty (2003). *Understanding MARC bibliographic: Machine readable cataloging.* Seventh edition reviewed and edited by the Network Development and MARC Standards Office, Library of Congress, Washington, DC. Library of Congress, The Follett Software Company (McHenry, IL). Available online <http://www.loc.gov/marc/umb/>.

Gookin, Dan (1998). *PCs for dummies.* Sixth edition. Foster City, CA: IDG Books Worldwide.

Gordon, Rachel Singer (2003). *The accidental systems librarian.* Medford, NJ: Information Today, Inc.

Greenstein, Daniel (2004). *Library stewardship in a networked age.* Available online <http://www.clir.org/pubs/reports/pub126/green.html>.

Hickey, Thomas B., Edward T. O'Neill, and Jenny Toves (2002). "Experiments with the IFLA Functional Requirements for Bibliographic Records (FRBR)." *D-Lib Magazine, 8* (9). Available online <http://www.dlib.org/dlib/september02/hickey/09hickey.html>.

Hilyer, Lee Andrew (2002). *Interlibrary loan and document delivery in the larger academic library: A guide for university, research, and larger public libraries.* Binghamton, NY: The Haworth Press.

Hock, Randolph (2004). *The extreme searchers' Internet handbook: A guide for the serious searcher.* Medford, NJ: CyberAge Books.

Jones, Wayne, ed. (2003). *E-serials: Publishers, libraries, users, and standards.* Second edition. Binghamton, NY: The Haworth Press.

Jones, Wayne, Judith R. Ahronheim, and Josephine Crawford, eds. (2002). *Cataloging the Web: Metadata, AACR, and MARC* 21. Lanham, MD: Scarecrow Press.

Kao, Mary L. (2001). *Introduction to technical services for library technicians.* Binghamton, NY: The Haworth Press.

Large, Andrew, Lucy Tedd, and R.J. Hartley (1999). *Information seeking in the online age: Principles and practice.* London: Bowker-Saur.

Lee, Stuart D. (2002). *Building an electronic resource collection: A practical guide.* London: Library Association.

Lee, Sul H., ed. (2002). *Impact of digital technology on library collections and resource sharing.* Binghamton, NY: The Haworth Press.

Libdex—Worldwide index of library catalogs (2004). Available online <http://www.libdex.com/>.

Library of Congress (2002). *MARC 21 Format for Holdings Data,* Concise edition. Available online <http://www.loc.gov/marc/holdings/>.

Library of Congress Portals Applications Issues Group (LCPAIG) (2004). Available online <http://www.loc.gov/catdir/lcpaig/paig.html>.

LibraryHQ.com (2004). *Library Automation/Technology Glossary.* Available online <http://www.libraryhq.com/glossary.html>.

Lipow, Anne Grodzins (2003). The librarian has left the building—but to where? In Heise, Jennifer and Stacey Kimmel (Eds.), *Virtual reference services: Issues and trends.* Binghamton, NY: The Haworth Press.

Lynch, Clifford A. (2000). From automation to transformation: Forty years of libraries and information technology in higher education. *EDUCAUSE Review,* January/February: 60-68.

Lynch, Clifford A. (June 2001). The battle to define the future of the book in the digital world. *First Monday, 6* (6). Available online <http://firstmonday.org/issues/issue6_6/ lynch/index.html>.

Lynch, Clifford A. (August 2001). Metadata harvesting and the open archives initiative. *ARL Bimonthly Report, 217.* Available online <http://www.arl.org/newsltr/217/mhp.html>.

Molyneux, Robert E. (2003). *The Internet under the hood: An introduction to network technologies for information professionals.* Westport, CT: Libraries Unlimited.

NISO Metasearch Initiative (2004). Available online <http://www.niso.org/committees/MS_initiative.html>.

NISO (2004). *OpenURL standard.* Available online <http://library.caltech.edu/openurl/>; <http://www.niso.org/committees/committee_ax.html>.

OCLC. *FRBR* [OCLC projects] (2004). Available online <http://oclc.org/research/projects/frbr/default.htm>.

OCLC. *xISBN* [OCLC projects] (2004). Available online <http://www.oclc.org/ research/projects/xisbn/>.

Ohio Library Council Diversity Awareness and Resources Committee (2004). *Adaptive Technology.* Available online <http://www.olc.org/diversity/adapt.html>.

Saffady, William (1999). *Introduction to library automation for librarians.* Fourth edition. Chicago: American Library Association.

Tennant, Roy (1999). User interface design: Some guiding principles, *Library Journal,* October 15. Available online http://www.libraryjournal.com/article/CA156510>.

Tennant, Roy, ed. (2002). *XML in libraries.* New York: Neal-Schuman Publishers.

Tracy, Joan I. (1986). *Library automation for library technicians: An introduction.* Metuchen, NJ: Scarecrow Press.

Unicode Home Page (2004). Available online <http://www.unicode.org/>.

University of Toronto. Adaptive Technology Resource Centre (2004). Available online *Technical Glossary.* <http://www.utoronto.ca/atrc/reference/tech/techgloss.html>.

Van de Sompel, Herbert and Oren Beit-Arie (2001). Open linking in the scholarly information environment using the OpenURL framework. *D-Lib Magazine, 7* (3), March. Available online <http://www.dlib.org/dlib/march01/vandesompel/03vandesompel.html>.

W3Schools online tutorials (2004). *XML tutorial.* Available online <http://www. w3schools.com/xml/ default.asp>.

Web Monkey HTML Cheatsheet (2004). Available online <http://hotwired.lycos. com/webmonkey/reference/html_cheatsheet/index.html>.

Webopedia: Online computer dictionary for computer and Internet terms and definitions (2004). Available online <http://www.webopedia.com/>.

Wurster, Christian (2002). *Computers. An illustrated history.* Koln, London: Taschen.

The XML FAQ (2004). Available online <http://www.ucc.ie/xml/>.

Index

Page numbers followed by the letter "f" indicate figures; those followed by the letter "t" indicate tables.